Economic Consequences of Divorce in Korea

Economic Consequences of Divorce in Korea

By

Hyunjin Kim

BRILL

LEIDEN | BOSTON

Library of Congress Control Number: 2016940156

Typeface for the Latin, Greek, and Cyrillic scripts: "Brill". See and download: brill.com/brill-typeface.

ISBN 978-90-04-32371-1 (paperback)
ISBN 978-90-04-32372-8 (e-book)

Originally published as Volume 1(1) 2016, in *Family Law in a Global Society*
DOI 10.1163/24058386-12340001.

This book is printed on acid-free paper and produced in a sustainable manner.

Contents

List of Tables and Figures

Tables

Figures

Economic Consequences of Divorce in Korea

Hyunjin Kim
Inha University School of Law, the Republic of Korea

Abstract

Still, the Korean divorce law adheres to fault-based divorce. According to the majority of Korean Supreme Court, the main reason of not admitting no-fault policy is that preconditions of systems for protecting the spouse and children after divorce financially are not yet satisfied in Korea. There have been remarkable development of divorce laws to pursue equality in property division between spouses, including re-conceptualizing pension entitlement as object of property division through Court's rulings and legislation. As to protect child after divorce, it is noteworthy to see a belated but wise establishment of the state agency to enforce child support obligations and its soft landing. However, we still have miles to go before the divorce laws secure true equality or fairness financially upon divorce.

Keywords

fault-based divorce – no-fault divorce – consensual divorce – equitable property division – pension entitlement – enforcement of child support

Part I Introduction

One of the wealthiest men in Korea has a child out of wedlock whom he has kept secret for several years. Then one day out of the blue, in a letter published in a national daily newspaper, he confesses to his love affair with another woman with whom he secretly has had a child, reveals the irretrievable breakdown of his marriage, and declares his intention to divorce his estranged wife. In response to the man's public confession, his wife makes clear her intention to save her marriage and keep her family intact, mentioning that their three grown-up children also do not want them to divorce. In such case, can the man get a judicial divorce against his estranged wife? The answer may come as a surprise in that in Korea it is unlikely that a judicial divorce would be granted to the husband in such case. It is interesting to note that this is a

 | DOI 10.1163/9789004323728-001

real case that is on-going, and those involved are high-profile individuals with celebrity status.[1]

In a recent en banc decision dated Sept. 15, 2015,[2] *Daebeobwon* [Supreme Court] affirmed the preexisting case law that does not allow a *Gajeong beobwon* [family court] to grant a judicial divorce in response to a petition by an at-fault spouse.[3] In a seven-to-six decision, the majority opinion argued that an at-fault spouse could have parted with his or her spouse through "consensual divorce" which is unique in Korea. It added that the ruling in favor of granting such petition for a judicial divorce could put the innocent spouse at risk, due to the absence under the present law of measures such as the hardship clause that financially protect the innocent spouse and children. Furthermore, the reality that the status of women is inferior to those of men in the Korean society should not be overlooked. With this decision, Korea remains one of the few countries that adhere to a fault-based divorce.

If we consider that the grounds upon which a divorce could be obtained are the product of the mores of society, Korea of the twenty-first century could be seen as quite conservative compared to other countries when it comes to divorce. This perception may lead to an inference that the freedom to divorce is limited in Korea and that the rate of divorce is low. However, this is not true. In Korea there are two types of divorce: "consensual divorce" and "judicial divorce." According to the Statistics Korea, in 2014 more than three quarters of divorce cases in Korea were by consensual divorce: the ratio of divorce by consensual divorce was 77.7%;[4] while there were 115,510 reported divorce cases, and only 25,800 of them were decided by judicial divorce. As the numbers show, the majority of couples ended their marriage by consensual divorce in Korea. Thus, it is apparent that the freedom to divorce is guaranteed by the system of consensual divorce in Korea. Moreover, Korea has a high divorce rate:

1 Dec. 29, 2015, *Se-Gye Ilbo*, The man is Choi Tae-won, the chairman of Korea's No. 3 conglomerate SK Group and his wife is Roh Soh-young, the daughter of former President of the Republic of Korea, Roh Tae-woo. They were married in 1988, and reportedly have been separated for a long time. The man's confessional letter was published in *Se-Gye Ilbo* on Dec. 26, 2015.

2 Supreme Court [S. Ct.], 2013Meu568, Sept. 15, 2015 (S. Kor.).

3 In this case, the claimant "A," got married to "B" in 1976 but had a love child with "C" in 1998. A left B in 2001 and he cohabited with C until he filed for divorce against B in 2011. B raised their three children by herself after A left them.

4 The ratio of the divorce by agreement in 2004 was 84.4%.

in 2014, the Crude Divorce Rate ("CDR")[5] was 2.3% and the Divorce Rate per Marriage[6] was 4.7%.[7] The trend of the increasing divorce rate in Korea is in line with that of other countries, evidenced by Korea's CDR of 2.3% in 2012, which is a little higher than the OECD average (Figure 1).[8] Globally nations have witnessed an increase in divorce rates, and divorce laws generally have focused on the consequences of divorce, e.g. compensating or distributing equally between divorcing parties and protecting the best interest of children after divorce.[9]

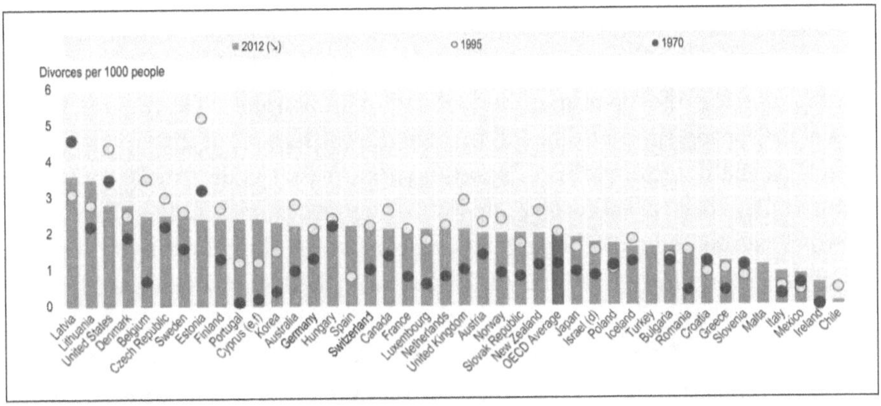

FIGURE 1 *World crude divorce rate, 1970, 1995 and 2012.*
SOURCE: OECD STATISTICS 2015, *AVAILABLE AT* HTTP://WWW.OECD.ORG/ELS/FAMILY/SF3_1_MARRIAGE_AND_DIVORCE_RATES.PDF

5 The crude divorce rate is the number of divorce cases that are dissolved each year per 1000 people.

6 Divorce Rate per Marriage is the number of divorce cases to the number of marriages in a given year (the ratio of the crude divorce rate to the crude marriage rate).

7 Statistics Korea, http://kosis.kr/eng/search/search01_List.jsp (last visited Jan. 10, 2016).

8 For the world divorce statistics of 2013—comparisons among countries, based on information collected by United Nations, see http://divorcescience.org/for-students/world-divorce-statistics-comparisons-among-countries/(last visited Jan. 10, 2016).

9 The Max Planck Encyclopedia of European Private Law, Vol. 1., 493 (Jurgen Basedow et al., ed., 2012).; Harry D. Krause, *Comparative family Law Past traditions battle future trends- and Vice versa*, in The Oxford Handbook of Comparative Law, 1113 (Reimann & Zimmermann eds., 2006).

Marriage, protected legally in Korea, is a contract formally entered into[10] by and between man and woman[11] of certain designated age.[12] This contract confers such man and woman a status of husband and wife, and it obligates husband and wife to live together, support and care for each other with exclusivity.[13] It creates a relationship of reciprocal obligations and rights, typically sharing "the fruit of marital partnership," that is, as an economic community, they establish their own family. Furthermore, as far as they give birth to a baby or adopt a baby, they are responsible for nurturing their own child as the child's custodians. Therefore, if this unit of community, a family, including their children, is dissolved by divorce, the question of how to settle, adjust and support this relationship after divorce cannot help but be important in social context. It is because these family units make up society, and divorce has continuing and life altering effects on members of such family units.[14] On the one hand, between spouses, such effects will involve the settlement of marital property, as well as the determination of spousal support that takes into account the "opportunity costs" that one gives up for managing a family. On the other hand, between parent and child, the effects will involve fulfilling the duty to support the child in the form of non-custodial parent's periodic payments to the custodial parent.

The divorce in Korea now is not the same as what it was in 1958 when the Korean Civil Code ("KCC") was first enacted. Customs and cultural attitudes related to divorce as well as those related to marriage have changed dramatically. There has been a remarkable development in the Korean divorce laws during the past fifty years. The jurisprudence regarding divorce has evolved by incorporating the case law whose decisions reflected the contemporaneous times, and by enacting a series of amendments to divorce laws in the KCC through the years. However, these changes and accomplishments would not have been possible if there was not a comparative study of family law. No one can deny that nations, despite their differences, face fundamentally similar

10 Nigel Lowe & Gillian Douglas, Bromley's Family Law 37 (2007).

11 It must be *heterosexual*; Korean law does not allow same-sex marriage as a legal marriage yet.

12 *Minbeob* [Civil Act], Act. No. 471, Feb. 22, 1958, art. 4 (S.Kor) (Majority) Majority is attained upon the completion of nineteen full years of age.
Art. 807 (Marriageable Age) Any person who is eighteen years old or older may enter into matrimony.
Art. 826-2 (Constructive majority) If a minor enters into marriage, he shall be deemed to have attained majority.

13 It must be *monogamous*. See art. 810 & 818 of KCC.

14 As to decline of living standard in divorced woman and the children after divorce, see generally Lenore J. Weitzman, The Divorce Revolution 318ff (1985).

questions and dilemmas in having to resolve problems related to divorce and family in modern times.[15] Therefore, the Korean courts and legislature cannot help but refer to other nations' decisions or laws through comparative study of family law. This is even more important in light of the fact that the Korean Civil Code was influenced by the laws of other nations, namely *Bürgerliches Gesetzbuch* [BGB][German Civil Code] and Code Civil [French Civil Code], and even the Japanese Civil Code as a result of the Japanese colonization of Korea. On the other hand, it is true that Korean divorce laws represent a mirror of the mores, culture, traditions and needs of the Korean society. Therefore, in an attempt to understand them, we need to look at Korean customs, the spirit of the times and Korean social structure.

It has been widely admitted that gender-based inequality obviously exists after divorce, although there are various differences in figures according to the researcher's approaches.[16] Painstaking empirical studies on the changes in occupations and incomes by work status, educational attainment and presence of minor children after divorce show that divorced women and their children suffer economic hardship unfairly and disproportionately in Korea as well.[17] Diagnosing and proposing a solution for structural discriminations in the labor market are beyond the scope of this article.

---

15 Since International Society of Family Law (ISFL) was founded in 1973, there have been a steady and significant worldwide interchange and close cooperation between family law scholars, judges, and practitioners led by this group. For ISFL's history, role and achievement, see Harry D. Krause, supra note 9, at 1102–1108.

16 For example, Weitzman suggested sensational findings that a 73 percent decline in women's standard of living after divorce and a 42 percent increase in men's standard of living (Weitzman, *supra* note 14, at 323). This result shocked the world and became one of the most cited demographic statistics of the 1980s. Weitzman argued that these economic consequences of divorce are due to no-fault divorce and other reforms introduced in California in 1970s. For critiques on her findings, see Hoffman, Saul & Duncan Greg, *What Are the Economic Consequences of Divorce?, in* Demography, 25:641–645 (1988); see also Peterson, Richard R., *A Re-Evaluation of the Economic Consequences of Divorce, in* American Sociological Review 61: 528–536 (1996)). For Weitzman's response to critiques, see Lenore J. Weitzman, *The Economic Consequences of Divorce Are Still Unequal: Comment On Peterson, in* American Sociological Review 61: 537–538 (1996). Although Weitzman admitted error in estimating data, resulting in exaggerated numbers, it cannot be denied that her findings had a real impact on public policy as well as on legal reforms.

17 See generally Kim Hye-young et al., *Yeoseongui Ihongwa Bingon: Jikeobgwa Sodeukui ByeonhwareulJungsimeuro* [*Women's Divorce and Poverty: Focusing on the changes in occupations and incomes*], *in* Gajokgwa Munhwa [Family and Culture], No. 20–2, 37–63 (2008). This study points out that divorced women are compelled to deal with low status, instability and chronic low wages, and makes a conclusion that "feminization of poverty" does not result from women's human capital, but from structural discriminations in the labor

The aim of this article is to develop an understanding of the economic consequences of divorce in Korea by analyzing Korean divorce laws, court rulings, and dispute resolution mechanisms. To accomplish this task, the overall structure of the article takes the form of six chapters, including an introduction (Chapter I) and a conclusion (Chapter VI). In establishing divorce laws, a balance between the freedom to divorce or benefit from divorce and the socio-economic loss to the spouse who is filed suit for divorce and children should be considered. These considerations are reflected through reasonable control of condition or process in getting divorce (Chapter III), fair division of marital property and damages upon divorce between the spouses (Chapter IV), and proper allocation and enforcement of child support responsibility (Chapter V). Based on the analysis of present economic consequences of divorce in Korean divorce laws, this article will propose future reforms for the unresolved problem related to Korean divorce laws (Chapter VI).

Part II Korean Customs and Laws on Divorce Revisited

I *Overview*

As Voltaire points out, "Divorce is probably of nearly the same date as marriage. I believe, however, that marriage is some weeks the more ancient,"[18] the history of divorce must go far back in the past, even though we cannot confirm it in Korean history. In western countries, the Roman law allowed divorce, but nations were able to prohibit or strictly regulate divorce under the Catholic principle of "indissolubility of marriage."[19] In Korea, under Confucianism, there was no concept of divorce. Rather the husband was allowed to repudiate[20] or abandon the wife under certain conditions. That meant the right to dissolve

---

market and the burden of rearing; See also Byun Wha-soon et al., Ihon hu Yeoseongui Sahoegyeongjejeok Jiwibyeonhwa [Changing of Women's Socio-economic Status after Divorce], Hangukyeoseonggaebalyeonguwon (2006).

18 François-Marie Voltaire, Dictionnaire philosophique, 23 (Alain Pons ed., Gallimand 1994) (1764).

19 "What therefore God hath joined together, let no *man* put asunder." See Matthew 19: 3, Luke, 16: 18, and Mark, 10: 9.

20 Charles Baron De Montesquieu, The Spirit of the Laws, 260 (Thomas Nugent trans., Cosimo Classics 2011) (1784). The difference between a divorce and a repudiation is that the former is made by mutual consent, arising from a mutual discontent; while the latter is formed by the will, and for the advantage of one of the two parties, independent of the will and advantage of the other.

a marriage did not belong to the wife, but to the husband, in the patriarchal Korean society. There was a thorough inequality between husband and wife.

Divorce laws reflect the spirit of the times and the social structure that rules that society.[21] Before reviewing the diachronic change of divorce laws in Korea, it would be helpful to consider Oliver Wendell Homes' words as follows:

> [In using] the history of our law as far as it is necessary to explain a conception or to interpret a rule, [...] there are two errors equally to be avoided both by writer and reader. One is that of supposing, because an idea seems very familiar and natural to us, that it has always been so. Many things which we take for granted have had to be laboriously fought out or thought out in the past times. The other mistake is the opposite one of asking too much of history. We start with man full grown. It may be assumed that the earliest barbarian whose practices are to be considered, had a good many of the same feelings and passions as ourselves.[22] [...] The customs, beliefs or the needs of a primitive time establish a rule or a formula. In the course of centuries, the custom, beliefs, or necessity disappears, but rule remains. The reason which gave rise to the rule has been forgotten, and ingenious minds set themselves to inquire how it is to be accounted for.[23]

Historically, the KCC has engaged in the reception of "western" laws. However, the traditions and customs relating to divorce in Chosŏn Dynasty during the nineteen century and in the Japanese colonial period during 1910 to 1945 had considerable influence in shaping Korean divorce laws in the KCC. Furthermore, these deep-rooted influences still play a role in interpretation of Korean divorce laws today. The current meaning of divorce in 2016 Korea is not the same as its meaning when the KCC was first enacted in 1958. There indeed has been a remarkable development in Korean divorce laws during the past fifty years. The Korean courts have continued to incorporate in its interpretation of Korean divorce laws the prevailing attitudes of the times, and accordingly a series of amendments to Korean divorce laws have been made. We review the Korean customs and laws on marriage and divorce in order to

---

21 See Cheong Ji-Won, *Chosŏnshidae Ihu Han'gugŭi Ihonjedoe Taehan Ilgoch'al [A Study on the Divorce System of Korea after Chosŏn Dynasty -Focusing mainly on the Causes of the Divorce and Gender Equality-]*, *in* Kajokpŏbyŏn'gu [Korean Journal of Family Law], Vol. 27-2, 139 (2013).

22 Oliver Wendell Homes, Jr., The Common Law 2 (1881).

23 *Id.*, at 5.

understand the current state of Korean divorce laws and of Korean people's attitudes regarding marriage and divorce.

II *The Influence of Confucianism in* Chosŏn *Dynasty*

A Marriage as a Transaction between Two Kin Groups

The Chosŏn Dynasty, the Korean last dynasty, lasted for about five hundred years from 1392 to 1910. The conspicuous characteristic of the Korean society in the late Chosŏn Dynasty was "kinship system that rested on highly structured patrilineal descendent groups."[24] This lineage culture was closely interconnected with Confucianism, the ideology whose norms and values would shape state and society.[25]

In the Chosŏn Dynasty, marriage was looked upon as uniting two families with strong legal, economic and political connotations, rather than as uniting man and woman.[26] For a structured patrilineal society, the obvious purpose of marriage was to produce a male offspring. Marriage was intended to be a bond between two families, with view to guarantee uninterrupted continuation of the husband's family lineage, honoring ancestors through rituals in ancestral temples and producing offspring.[27] The married couple should reside virilocally. Thus, people used to think that a married daughter was so-called "*Chulgaoiin*," which means no longer a member of their own family. It would be exceedingly interesting that the terminology "*Sijipkada*" the Korean verb which corresponds to "she gets married," literally means "go to her parents-in-law's house." A daughter-in-law was given the keys to her husband's family barn and should live together with her parents-in-law performing their ancestral worshiping rituals as well as caring for her parents-in-law. Thus, a woman could get social standing in society only through marriage and the wife was supposed to assume leadership in this domestic realm. Her heavy responsibility was to keep the peace and prosperity for her husband's family. There was an old expression that if a woman marries into a family, she should be a ghost of her husband's family even after her death. These traditional customs on marriage have brought on barriers to divorce for married women.

---

24 Martina Deuchler, The Confucian Transformation of Korea, A study of Society and Ideology 24 (1992).

25 Thus, ancient China's canonical literatures, like the *Ye-ki* (Book of Rites), the *Ui-rhe* (Book of Etiquettes and ceremonies) and *Chou-rhe* (Book of beurocracy), in which models for perfect ritual behavior and a sound sociopolitical order was contained, had functioned as social criteria.

26 Martina Deuchler, *supra* note 24, at 236.

27 *Id.*, at 237. The first sentence of the chapter on marriage in the *Ye-ki* (Book of Rites) testifies to this.

B Dissolution of Marriage

Unilateral Expelling of Wife: Ch'ilgŏjiak and Sambulgŏ

In the Chosŏn Dynasty, influenced heavily by Confucian thinking, a wife could not demand dissolution of marriage, which only a husband could declare unilaterally.[28] A husband could legitimately reject his wife and force her out of the house for the reason that his wife committed one of the seven sins. Koreans refer to these seven sins as "*Ch'ilgŏjiak or Ch'ilchul*" (the seven evils for expulsion), and they are the following: 1) disobedience towards the parents-in-law, 2) failure to give birth to a son, 3) engaging in lewd behavior, 4) undue jealousy, 5) grave illness, 6) extreme talkativeness, and 7) stealing.

However, even if a wife committed one of these seven conditions, her husband could not expel his wife if she met one of the conditions called "*Sambulgŏ*" (three situations for not expelling a wife). These conditions were as follows: 1) if the wife went through three years of mourning for the death of either of the husband's parents, 2) if the wife went through economic difficulties with the husband and the family fortune improved with her sacrifice or aid, or 3) the wife had no place to return after the dissolution of marriage. These were the stipulations that prevented the abuse in the application of the seven sins.

The interesting point is that none of the laws in Chosŏn Dynasty clearly prescribed the causes or processes for dissolution of marriage.[29] The *Kyongkuktaejon* [the Chosŏn's Code] applying the *Taemyŏngnyul* [The Great Ming Code of China] was a general law in criminal field,[30] and *Taemyŏngnyul* provided the provisions for punishing the husband who acted improperly in expelling his wife. It is presumed that the reason for not clearly prescribing such causes or processes for expulsion of wife is that the Chosŏn Dynasty, heavily steeped in Confucian ideals, seemed to recognize "the two sets of criteria for and against the expulsion of a wife as a means of moral pressure rather than as that of legal value."[31] The Chosŏn Dynasty treated a husband harshly if he expelled his wife without a grave reason specified in *Ch'ilgŏjiak*. If a husband

---

28 *Kyongkuktaejon*, art. 578–581.

29 See Chung Hae-eun, *Chosŏnhugi Ihonŭi Shilsanggwa Taemyŏngnyurŭi Chŏkyong* [*The Reality of divorce in the later half period of the Choson dynasty, and the application of the Grand Ming Cord*], *in* Chosŏnhugi Ihonŭi Shilsanggwa Taemyŏngnyurŭi Chŏkyong [History and Reality], No. 75, 110 (2010). Therefore, that had caused a public debate occasionally whether there was any stipulation relating to divorce in Chosŏn Dynasty when the government happened to decide on permission to divorce.

30 See Jung Kwanghyun, Han'gukkajokpŏbyŏn'gu [Korean Law of Family Relations and Successions] 5 (Seoul University Press, INC. 1967); see generally Cho Jeeman, *Chosŏn sidaeeul hyoungsabeob-Daemyounglyulkwa kukjeon*-[The Ming Code and the National Code as Criminal Law in the Chosŏn Dynasty] 31 (Kyounginmunhwasa 2007).

31 Martina Deuchler, *supra* note 24, at 273.

expelled his wife without having proof of one of the seven sins, or disregarded the three exceptions, he was sentenced to eighty strokes of caning, and the *Puhap* order to recover the marriage was given. Even though the spousal relationship had already irretrievably dissolved, and smooth conjugal life could not be expected, the State allowed neither repudiation nor divorce, and this was regarded as rehabilitation.

A husband had a discretionary power over his wife's status as a dignified wife. He was not punished for not expelling his wife, even though his wife committed one of the seven sins, and therefore he did not need to expel his disobedient wife. Thus, he was authorized to keep or expel his disobedient wife. Therefore, the threat of the husband expelling the wife from his family and the fear of a social stigma attached to being an expelled wife functioned very well as a way of making women obedient and submissive throughout their marriage.[32]

Compulsory Expulsion: Uijŏl

On the other hand, there was a compulsory expulsion called '*Uijŏl*' [disowning]. If a husband or a wife committed one of the grounds for *Uijŏl*, he or she was forced to divorce. Unless he or she was divorced, the government had to punish the couple and let the couple divorce necessarily without considering their intentions. The gender-inequality related to the grounds of *Uijŏl* is specially worth noting.[33] First, the grounds applied to a wife were as follows: when a wife committed adultery; when she swore hard or battered her parents-in-law (or her grandparents-in-law) or injured or murdered her parents-in-law (or any of her husband's relatives); when she committed misconduct to any of her husband's relatives, or when she tried to kill her husband. While, different grounds applied to a husband, when a husband made his wife commit adultery or sold his wife as another man's concubine, when he battered his parents-in-law (or his grandparents-in-law) or murdered his parents-in-law (or any of his relatives), when he committed misconduct with her mother-in-law. If we consider how widely the verbs "swear hard" and "injure" could be interpreted, the grounds against a wife seem to be unfairly disadvantageous. Also, if a wife committed adultery, compulsory expulsion was applied; but if a husband committed adultery, compulsory expulsion did not apply and he was not punished.

---

32 *Id.*

33 See generally, Chung Hae-eun, *supra* note 29, at 98; see also Chang Byung-In, *Chosŏnshidae Ihone Taehan Kyujewa Kŭ Shilsang* [*The Regulation and Real Facts of Divorce in Chosŏn Period*], *in* Minsok'akyŏn'gu [Folklore Study] 28 (1999).

Summary

To sum up, the policy on dissolution of marriage during Chosŏn Dynasty was aimed at discouraging such dissolution in order to maintain the order in society, and despite this policy, when the expulsion of the wife from her husband's household occurred, there were no protective measures for the wife to ably deal with financial and social hardship.[34]

III *The Influence of the Japanese Colonization*

A Application of Korean Customs from 1912 to 1922

After the Japan-Korean Annexation Treaty in 1910, the Japanese colonial government issued *Chosŏn Minsaryong* (the Civil Ordinance), to take effect on April 1, 1912. The Ordinance announced that most of civil matters should be governed by the Japanese Civil Code, the Japanese Civil Procedure Code, and the Japanese Commercial Code. However, it was declared that the significant part of private law among Koreans be regulated by Korean customary rules through Article 9 to 11 of the Ordinance; thus the matters of capacity, family and succession, and real property rights were decreed to be governed by Korean customs instead of Japanese law. This decision was based on the judgment that Korean traditional practices on family including marriage, divorce, adoption and succession were seriously different from the Japanese Civil Code, considering he Korean Customs Survey Report (Kwansŭpchosabogosŏ) conducted by the Japanese colonial government.[35] For this reason, the Chosŏn Dynasty's customs functioned as a rule on marriage and divorce, and therefore, we have to turn to reviewing the Korean customs mentioned above.

B Application of Japanese Civil Code from 1923 to 1945

The Korean society in 1920's witnessed a proliferation of divorce cases. According to press reports, the divorce rate skyrocketed in 1920's.[36] These

---

34 Chang Byung-in, *supra* note 33, at 30.

35 Kukyŏk Kwansŭpchosabogosŏ [The Reports on the Korean Customs], 354 (No. 134) (Han'gukpŏpcheyŏn'guwŏn 1992). The translations of the "Kwansŭpchosabogosŏ," were published in 1910, 1912, and 1913 based on the Japanese systematic and nationwide research from May 1908 to September 1910. However, this Korean Customs Survey Report had limits in two ways: one is that Korean customs were investigated from the Japanese point of view as foreigners, and the other one is that there could have been distortion of truth for the purpose of colonizing. Kaeyŏkp'an Kwansŭpchosabogosŏ, Preface.

36 For example, in *Dong-a ilbo*, one of the Korean three nation-wide newspapers, had reported the divorce problems in full, under the pungent titles of "Divorce by consent, an epidemic of family breakdown" on June 26, 1922, and "the country village families are disrupted by buying and selling wives, getting divorce by consent on the slightest provocation" on March 17, 1928.

changes could be explained by two reasons. On the one hand, the Japanese colonial government changed the policy to apply the Japanese Civil Code in governing divorce between Koreans by revising the Civil Ordinance in 1922. Therefore, "consensual divorce" and "judicial divorce" of the Japanese Civil Code that did not apply previously to divorce was introduced to Korea starting on July 1, 1923. On the other hand, as enlargement of educational opportunity to girls, development of women's autonomy, liberation of female-gender were manifested by diverse levels of people and on various way of media, problems on families and women came to the forefront of reform in 1920s.[37] The advent of new women like flappers in western countries had influence on a variety of different fields including divorce.

Consensual Divorce

The Article 11–2 of the Revised Civil Ordinance prescribed that "consensual divorce" shall take effect upon reporting to mayors of cities, towns, or villages. Interestingly, Japanese legislators had created the system of "consensual divorce" in 1894, when the Japanese Civil Code was established, modeling it after the French Civil Code.[38] "Consensual divorce" was not based on the Japanese tradition, which only allowed a husband's unilateral expulsion of his wife. Then, why did legislators invent "consensual divorce" in the Japanese Civil Code? The reason was universally accepted as a way for allowing husband's "unilateral repudiation" under the guise of "liberal divorce by couple's consent,"[39] and the same recognition was given in Korea. As the result, the wife, the social and economic weak party, could be forced to divorce too easily through the husband reporting "consensual divorce" to the mayor of a city, village or town, without any countermeasure after divorce or any division of property upon divorce.

Judicial Divorce

Article 813 of the Japanese Civil Code, which was made to apply to the Korean people, listed the causes for judicial divorce as follows: (a) the other spouse's bigamy, (b) a wife's adultery, (c) a husband's punishment on adultery, (d) the

37 See generally, Kwon Hee Jung, *Shikminji sidae hankook kagokeui byunhwa* [*The Change of Korean Family in the Colonial Period focusing on Divorce Case*], *in* Bikyomunhwa younku, 11–2, 35–82 (2005).

38 Yune Jinsu ed., Chuhaech'inchokpŏp, Vol. 1, 442 (Pakyŏngsa 2015).

39 See Herald Fuess, Divorce in Japan, Family, Gender, and the State, 1600–2000, 109 (2004); see also Kim Joo-soo & Kim Sang-yong, Ch'injoksangsokpŏp [Family Law], 163 (Beopmunsa, 11 ed., 2013).

other spouse's gross criminal penalties, (e) the other spouse's extreme maltreatment, (f) the other spouse's malicious abandonment, (g) the parents-in-law's extreme maltreatment, (h) the other spouse's extreme maltreatment to the parents-in-law, and (i) the death or life of other spouse has been unknown for three years.

This provision of the Japanese Civil Code, however, was revised and was incorporated into Article 770. The law as amended in 1947, having deleted (g) and (h), and inserted a general and abstract clause, "if there exists any other serious cause for making it difficult to continue the marriage." Furthermore, this revision led to a turning point in divorce policy from fault-based divorce to no fault divorce, through the Japanese courts' application of the abstract clause affirmatively in cases. However, this reform was made after Korea's liberation in 1945 and it did not affect Korea.

New Cases of Divorce by Women

As for new cases of divorce by women, there are two noteworthy cases to mention. The two cases had several things in common: The women involved were highly intelligent and promising individuals and graduated from the same girls high school; they married to famous men, giving birth to children; and their divorce caused a national scandal. The first woman, Pahk Induk, an elite who graduated from Ewha Women's University and had studied abroad, was known as the first woman who paid compensation to her husband when they divorced in 1931, even though she was not at fault. Her husband, who had been born into wealth, went bankrupt one year after he was married to Pahk and did not work after bankruptcy, forcing Pahk to solely support the family and in-laws by teaching at schools day and night. After six years of a hard married life, Pahk went abroad to study alone in the U.S. through a scholarship, leaving her two daughters to be cared for by her mother-in-law. On returning after another six years of studying, she unilaterally declared her intention to divorce her husband and not return to her status as wife. On her husband's demand of money in exchange of his consent to divorce, she reluctantly paid him the amount requested. After divorce, she established an agricultural high school as well as a university in Korea, and became a well-known author in the U.S. for her autobiographies written in the English language.[40]

The second woman, Na Hyesuk, a famous painter who had studied abroad in Japan, was the first woman to file a damages claim against her lover with whom

40 Induk Pahk, September Monkey (NY Harper & Brothers, 1954); Induk Pahk, The Hour of the Tiger (NY Harper & Brothers, 1954); Induk Pahk, The Cock Still Crows (Vantage Press, Incorporated, 1977).

she had had an affair during her marriage, after she divorced in 1934.[41] She fell in love with a Korean religious leader, Choi Lynn, whom she happened to meet while traveling around the world with her husband, a diplomat, and her infidelity was exposed as the result of the her lover's public boasting. Compelled to divorce penniless, she suffered extreme poverty and was kept away from her children, longing for them her entire life. She published "Written Confession of Divorce" in a major newspaper as a way to overcome her trials and tribulations. However, it made her situation more even difficult and had a rippling negative effect. Finally, she passed away on the road alone and penniless. Her son, a law professor in the U.S., later published a book on his biological mother.[42]

No one can deny that these two divorce cases were extraordinary at that times. The media reported marital lives of new generation of women and their actions to file for divorce in detail, and this peep into these women's lives had a profound impact on the public.

IV *Korean Civil Code of 1958*

Adoption of Other Laws

The KCC was enacted in 1958 and came into force on January 1, 1960.[43] The National Committee of Civil Code had referred to other countries' civil codes, such as the German BGB, the French Civil Code, the Swiss Code and the Japanese Civil Code etc., in making the KCC. Thus, the KCC follows the continental legal system: Historically, the KCC has incorporated the laws of other nations, including those of BGB, the Code Napoleon, the Japanese Civil Code, and have actively referred to them in enacting and amending the KCC.

Patriarchal Characters

On the one hand, many provisions on marriage and divorce in the KCC as enacted in 1958 reveal its patriarchal character. For example, a wife is required to live with her husband in his residence, because the husband has the right to designate the place of residence (art. 826(2), KCC of 1958). Only the husband is responsible for the expenses necessary for communal life (article 833), and thus automatically the husband is presumed to be the master of any property, whose title is uncertain even under a separate property system. As to parental authority of a minor child, during marriage principally the father becomes the custodian; after divorce, only the father has the parental right (article 909④)

41 September 20, 1934, *Dong-a ilbo*.

42 Jin Kim & Yontaek Lee, *Geu Ttaen Geu Giri Wae I-ri Jobatdeongo* [Why the road was so narrow then?] (Haenuri 2009).

43 *Minbeob* [Civil Code], Act. No. 471, Feb. 22, 1958 (S. Kor.)

and the divorced mother could not even meet her children after divorce because the visitation right was not allowed.

Element of Gender Equality

On the other hand, there was progress in terms of gender equality. First, all the causes for judicial divorce in the KCC of 1958, including an act of unchastity, are aimed at both husband and wife equally (the subparagraph 1 of article 840 of KCC). Therefore, a wife can dissolve her marriage in filing a divorce suit against her husband on the ground that he has had an affair. Second, when a marriage has been dissolved one party may claim against the at-fault party damages for pain and suffering (article 806 of KCC), and therefore a wife could use her right to consent that is necessary for "consensual divorce" as a leverage to receive more compensation. However, the claim for property division as a liquidation of marital property had been discussed by the National Assembly at the time of the enactment of the KCC in 1958 but was not adopted at the time.

V *Amendments to Korean Family Laws in Korean Civil Code*

There has been a remarkable development in Korean divorce laws during the past fifty years. The family law part of the KCC is the most amended section in the KCC since the enactment of the KCC in 1958. Going through the amendments over the years is important in understanding and interpreting the present provisions. Accordingly I will review the major reforms relating to marriage and divorce in a chronological order.

The long-standing movement for reforming Korean family law achieved fruition in the remarkable reform of 1977.[44] The reform of 1977 included the following key provisions: A minor shall be deemed to have attained the age of majority, once he/she enters into marriage (art. 826-3). Any property, of which title is uncertain between husband and wife, shall be presumed to be in their co-ownership (art. 830(2)). As result of introducing joint parental authority, parental authority shall be jointly exercised by both parents during their marriage. But in that the father was allowed to exercise parental authority if the parents fail to reach an agreement, a problem of gender inequality still remained. It is noteworthy to point out that a condition for "consensual divorce" was included in the KCC of 1977 requiring that husband and wife must declare their true intention to divorce in front of a family court judge before proceeding with consensual divorce (art. 836).

---

44 Amended by Act. No. 3051, Dec. 31, 1977.

The most fundamental and important reform on marriage and divorce was introduced in 1990.[45] The following are some of the key provisions in the amended KCC of 1990. The provision recognizing a claim for division of property was introduced in order to protect the divorced spouse financially (art. 839). Matters concerning rearing children after divorce shall be determined by agreement (art. 837). The visitation rights are given to the parent who does not take care of the minor child after divorce (art. 837-2). During marriage, the place of residence shall be determined by agreement between husband and wife, and if they fail to reach an agreement, the family court shall determine it (article 826). The living expenses shall be jointly and severally borne by the couple (art. 833).

Further amendment to the Korean family law was made in 2005, and it was initiated by the Korean Constitutional Court decision that certain of its provisions are unconstitutional.[46] The amended KCC of 2005 abolished *Hoju-je* [the Head of the Family system] and modified *Tongsŏngdongbonburhon* [Same-Surname-Same Origin Marriage Ban]. The amended KCC of 2005 did away with the 6 month waiting period previously required for women to remarry after divorce. If the wife gave birth to a child during this period, the waiting period for remarriage ended upon the delivery date of the child. This condition was in place to ensure the paternity of a child born around the time of divorce.[47]

Strengthening the procedure for getting consensual divorce was the main achievement of the reform in 2007.[48] The amended KCC of 2007 introduced "reflection period" before the family court's confirmation, and required the couple to agree on the details of child rearing, including the custodian, the burden of child support expenses, and the way of exercising visitation rights (art. 837). Details of the procedures for getting a consensual divorce will be discussed in Chapter III. Furthermore, it allowed a minor child to have visitation rights (art. 837-2). A spouse's right to revoke fraudulent acts by the other

---

45 Amended by Act. No. 4199, Jan. 13, 1990.

46 Amended by Act. No. 7427, March 31, 2005.

47 As to remarriage ban on women after divorce, the United Nations Human Rights Committee (UNHRC) and the United Nations Committee on the Elimination of Discrimination against Women (CEDAW) recommended the abolishment in 1998 and in 2003 respectively. European countries, eg. German repealed it in 1998 and France in 2004. The Japanese Supreme Court, however, recently declared that the provision of prohibiting for six month is unconstitutional on the ground that more than 100 days is excessive. It is reportedly expected to revise the Japanese Code Civil from six months to 100 days. Dec. 16. 2015, *The Mainichi*.

48 Amended by Act. No. 8720, Dec. 21, 2007.

spouse was created to preserve the claim for equitable division of property (art. 839-3).

Additional reforms in 2009 introduced the content and procedures for child support enforcement system.[49] Details on such system will be discussed in Chapter V.

VI *Significant Family Law Rulings*

It is no exaggeration to say that a series of significant court rulings by the Korean Supreme Courts and the Korean Constitutional Court has been the driving force behind reforms in Korean family law. For important family law cases, the two Courts have reflected the changes of society, by abolishing the customs and traditions contrary to the gender equality. However, they endeavored to balance between the conservative and progressive approaches.

Korean Constitutional Court's Rulings

Hunbeob [the Korean Constitution] protects marriage and family life in article 36(1), in which "Marriage and family life shall be entered into and sustained on the basis of individual dignity and equality of the sexes, and the State shall do everything in its power to achieve that goal." However, there were several provisions potentially contrary to the Constitution, related to marital relation or divorce. In Some sense, "Reform of Korean Family Law was marked by struggles between the Constitutional principles and tradition.[50]

The Constitutional Court ruled that the article 809 of KCC,[51] *Tongsŏngdongbonburhon* [Same-Surname-Same Origin Marriage Ban], was not incompatible with the Constitution in 1997.[52] In Korea, a child takes his or her father's

49 See generally Jinsu Yune, *The Reform of the Consensual Divorce Process and the Child Support Enforcement System in Korea, in* Journal of Korean Law, vol. 11, 247–261 (2012).

50 See Jinsu Yune, *Tradition and the Constitution in the Context of the Korean Family Law, in* Journal of Korean Law, vol. 5, No. 1, 212 (2005).

51 Art. 809 of KCC was the codification of a traditional rule prohibiting marriage between men and women who have the same surname and ancestral home.

52 Constitutional Court [Const. Ct], July 16, 1997 (S. Kor.) The majority opinion stated that: the law against marriages between members of the same agnatic lineage descendants violates the dignity of human beings and the right to the pursuit of happiness as guaranteed by the Constitution as well as the right to free marriages and equality. The majority emphasized the individual's freedom of marriage and asserted that: majority of the public's concept of marriage has changed from one of "a union between families" to one of "a union between persons", reflecting the respect for a person's free will."

surname,[53] and according to article 809 of KCC, a man and a woman who have the same surnames were not permitted to marry. This provision was much criticized by lawyers and the Korean Law Association on the ground that it infringed on the freedom of choice in marriage, and that it reinforced traditional paternalism.[54] After this case, the National Assembly of South Korea passed an amendment to this provision in March 2002, which came into force on 31 March 2005, and now marriage may not be allowed only between a man and a woman who are closely related.[55]

Next, the Constitutional Court decided that *Hoju-je* [the Head of the Family system] was unconstitutional in 2005.[56] The deletion of *Hoju-je*, a vestige of a patriarchal system, meant that the Korean Society was transforming from a male-oriented society to an individual-oriented one irrespective of gender and shifting focus from a kin group-based family unit to a husband-and-wife based family unit.[57]

The Constitutional Court ruled that the anti-adultery provision, article 241 of the Criminal Act, is also unconstitutional in 2015.[58] This provision imposed

---

53 Art. 781(1) of KCC. However, an exception was introduced in 2002 reform: when the parents agree to have the child assume his or her mother's surname and origin of surname at the time of filing a report on their marriage, he or she shall succeed the mother's surname and origin of surname.

54 For the argument in detail, see generally, Jinsu Yune, *supra* note 34, at 200–203.

55 Art. 809 of KCC (Prohibition of Consanguineous Marriage, etc.)
(1) A marriage may not be allowed between blood relatives (including the blood relatives of an adoptee before full adoption) within the eighth degree of relationship.
(2) A marriage may not be allowed between the parties who are or were such relatives by affinity as the spouses of blood relatives within the sixth degree of relationship, the blood relatives of the spouse within the sixth degree of relationship, and the spouses of blood relatives of the spouse within the fourth degree of relationship.
(3) A marriage may not be allowed between the parties who were the blood relatives of adoptive parent line within the sixth degree of relationship and the affinity relatives of adoptive parent line within the fourth degree of relationship.

56 Constitutional Court [Const. Ct], 2001Hun-ka9,10,1112,13,14,15, & 2004Hun-Ka5, Feb. 3, 2005 (S. Kor.), Jinsu Yune, *Chŏnt'ongjŏk Kajokchedowa Hŏnbŏp* [*Traditional family system and the Constitution*], *in* Minbŏpnon'go (IV) 89 (Pakyŏngsa 2009).

57 For the controversy of the 'head of the family' system and the effect of the abolition of it, see Whasook Lee, *Transformation of Korean Family Law*, *in* International Survey of Family Law 2008, 240–243 (B. Atkin ed, Jordan Publishing Limited, 2008); see also Jinsu Yune, *supra* note 34, at 204–207.

58 Constitutional Court [Const. Ct], 2009Hun-ba17·205, 2010Hun-ba194, 2011Hun-ba 4, 2012Hun-ba 57·255·411, 2013Hun-ba139·161·267·342·365, 2014Hun-ba53·464, 2011Hun-ka31, 2014Hun-ka4 (Consolidated). Feb. 26, 2015 (S. Kor.).

imprisonment as the only statutory sentence in the criminal punishment of adultery or fornication with a married person.[59]

En Banc Decisions of the Korean Supreme Court

Regarding the division of marital assets upon divorce, the Korean Supreme Court clarified the nature of property division. First, the Supreme Court addressed the division of marital property for a couple with more debt than assets in an en banc decision dated June 20, 2013.[60] In this 8 to 5 decision, the majority opinion overruled the preexisting case law, which held that one spouse's property division claim is rejected where another spouse has debts and nothing is left after the deduction of such debts from the total property.[61]

Second, in a series of en banc decisions on July 16, 2014, the Supreme Court enlarged the scope of marital assets subject to property division by including a public official's retirement and pension entitlements. This issue was so important that the process of public defense was broadcast live to the nation.[62] The majority opinion of the Korean Supreme Court overruled the preexisting case law, which excluded a public official's retirement and pension entitlements from the marital assets subject to property division upon divorce and rather took it into account as a mere "other circumstance" for evaluating contents and methods of property division, for the reason that the remaining life span of the spouse receiving entitlements cannot be confirmed.[63] The Supreme Court held that when the retirement and pension entitlements are divided by periodic payments, it is reasonable to ascertain division proportion individually by distinguishing such entitlements from other general properties.[64]

Last but not least, the Supreme Court affirmed the preexisting case law that does not allow a family court to grant a judicial divorce in response to a

59 Interestingly, the Court previously ruled this article constitutional four times on September 10, 1990, March 11, 1993, October 25, 2001 and October 30, 2008 respectively (89Hun-Ma82, 90Hun-Ka70, 2000Hun-ba60, and 2007Hun-ka17·221, 2008Hun-ka7·26, 2008Hun-ba21·47 (Consolidated).

60 Supreme Court en banc Decision 2010Meu4071,4088, June 20, 2013 (S. Kor.).

61 Supreme Court [S. Ct.] 97Meu933, Sept. 26, 1997 (S. Kor.); Supreme Court [S. Ct.] 2001Meu718, Sept. 4, 2002 (S. Kor.) etc.

62 See the video on June 19, 2014 available at http://www.scourt.go.kr/supreme/media/MediaActivityViewAction.work?gubun=710&currentPage=&pageSize=9&seqnum=4.

63 Supreme Court en banc Decision 2013Meu2250, July 16, 2014 (S. Kor.).

64 Supreme Court en banc Decision 2012Meu2888, July 16, 2014 (S. Kor.). https://library.scourt.go.kr/kor/judgment/eng_judg_view.jsp.

petition by at-fault spouse, in an en banc decision on September 15, 2015,[65] as we will discuss the arguments later in the next chapter.

Part III Procedures and Grounds for Divorce

I *Overview*

Korea is one of the few countries that adhere to the fault-based divorce policy.[66] Some practitioners insist that the "consensual divorce" that is unique in Korea lowers the pressure for no-fault divorce. Korean divorce laws provide two types of divorce, consensual divorce and judiciary divorce.[67] A consensual divorce involves dissolution of marriage without the court's judgment and can be obtained as long as both spouses agree on the terms of divorce. In contrast, a judicial divorce is achieved by the court's decision when a spouse applies to the family court for divorce based on one of the prescribed grounds for divorce and succeeds in proving it. The characteristics of judicial divorce compared to consensual divorce in Korea could be explained by the following: lack of agreement to divorce; initiation of the judicial procedure; and evidentiary proof of one of the grounds for divorce prescribed by law. In practice the rate of consensual divorce is overwhelmingly higher to that of judiciary divorce.

The provisions on "consensual divorce" in the KCC were modeled after those in the Japanese Civil Code, which appears to have been independently enacted by the Japanese legislature rather than being derived from the French Civil Code. The KCC, enacted in 1958, has been derived from the laws of other nations, namely those of the German Civil Code, the French Civil Code and the Japanese Civil Code. However, the Korean system concerning divorce and its processes is ingenious in several ways.

First, the procedures for consensual divorce under Korean law are simpler than ones from other nations: The process only requires that the couple agree

---

65 Supreme Court [S. Ct.], 2013Meu568, Sept. 15, 2015 (S. Kor.).

66 European countries introduced "no-fault grounds for divorce": Netherlands and UK in 1971, Italy in 1975, France in 1976, and Ireland in 1997. No-fault divorce is allowed in all fifty states and the District of Columbia in U.S.: on August 10, 2010 the governor of New York signed a no-fault divorce Bill at last, more than forty years later when California adopted a no-fault divorce in Family Law Act of 1969.

67 Strictly speaking, there are three types of divorce in Korea, in the base that a conciliation is preliminary to a divorce suit; A spouse wishing to file for divorce to the family court, shall first make a request for conciliation; When a divorce suit has been instituted without making a request for conciliation, the family court shall refer the relevant case to conciliation (*Kasa sosongbeob* [Family Procedure Act] Act. No. 4300, Dec. 31, 1990, art. 50 (S. Kor.)).

on divorce and that the court issue a certificate after confirming this consent. Because it was considered that the ease of the process promoted and encouraged consensual divorce, the procedural requirements were amended after 50 years since their establishment. We will later review the unique characteristics of the Korean consensual divorce system and the recent amendments to it, comparing it with the consensual divorce systems in other countries, especially one in France.

Second, there are six grounds for judicial divorce under the KCC, and these have not been altered since their enactment in 1958. The fault grounds could be categorized into three groups: the first group includes unchastity, malicious desertion and an instance when it is unconfirmed as to whether the missing spouse is dead or alive; the second group reflects the customs and culture of Korea, relating to the maltreatment of a spouse or his/her parents by another spouse; the last one is abstract, which is "any other serious cause for making it difficult to continue the marriage." There is no provision that limits only a spouse that is without fault to file for divorce, but the courts have ruled firmly that only an innocent spouse could petition for divorce. Even though an at-fault spouse proves that there is an irreconcilable difference between the couple, the court would not permit judicial divorce.[68] However, there are exceptional cases as we shall see later in this chapter. We will generally analyze the grounds and review the arguments concerning the fault-based divorce.

II *Consensual Divorce: Freedom to Divorce*

Need for Reform

More than three quarters of divorce cases in Korea are processed through consensual divorce, as commented above: The ratio of consensual divorce reached 84.4% in 2004; but it decreased to 77.7% in 2014 (Figure 2).[69] The number of consensual divorces declined by 14.3 thousand to 90.8 thousand cases in 2008, whereas the number of judicial divorces was 25.8 thousand cases in 2008, which rose by 6.9 thousand cases from the previous year (Table 1).

What has brought this decrease in the rate of consensual divorce since 2007? The amendment to the KCC regarding the procedures for consensual divorce was one of the fundamental reasons. The pre-reform consensual divorce process

68 Japan Court has ruled for at-fault spouse to file for divorce suit, even though the Japanese Civil Code has the similar provision of abstract ground for judicial divorce as that of Korean. As to the discussion on this issue at the code review committee in 1896. See generally Herald Fuess, *supra* note 39, at 112.

69 According to the Statistics Korea, *available at* http://kosis.kr/eng/search/search01_List.jsp (last visited October 16, 2015).

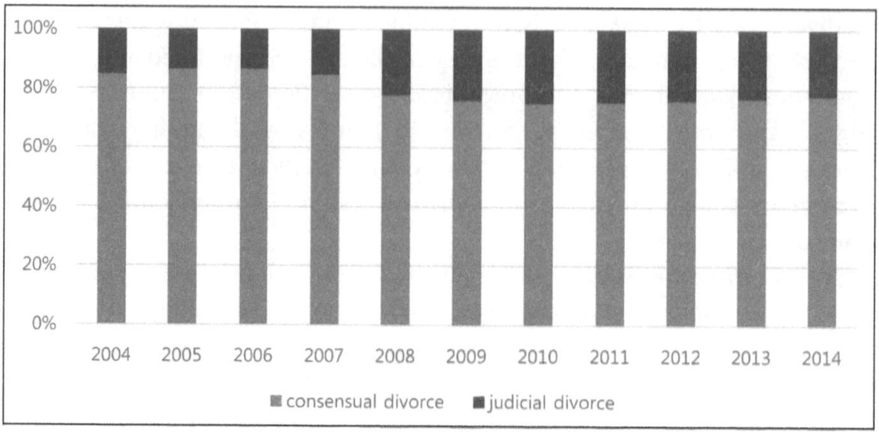

FIGURE 2 *Ratio of divorce by type.*
SOURCE: STATISTICS KOREA, MARRIAGE AND DIVORCE STATISTICS IN 2014, 21 (2015).

TABLE 1 *Number of divorces by type 2003–2014* (Unit: 1,000)

Year	Total number of divorces	Consensual divorce	Judiciary divorce
2003	166.6	143.2	22.3
2004	138.9	117.3	21
2005	128.0	110.7	16.4
2006	124.5	107.9	16.4
2007	124.1	105.1	18.9
2008	116.5	90.8	25.8
2009	124.0	94.4	29.6
2010	116.9	87.8	29.0
2011	114.3	86.4	27.8
2012	114.3	86.9	27.4
2013	115.3	88.6	26.6
2014	115.5	89.7	25.8
Percent change	0.2	1.3	-3.3

SOURCE: STATISTICS KOREA, MARRIAGE AND DIVORCE STATISTICS IN 2004, 21 (2015).

was very simple: the consent by the couple to divorce was the only necessary and sufficient condition. If a husband and a wife agree to divorce voluntarily, they would go to the family court together and show their intention to divorce in front of a judge. Then, the court would issue a certificate after the judge verifies the veracity of the couple's intention to divorce. What the couple had to do was to jointly sign on the report and obtain signatures of another two adult witnesses (art. 836 of KCC). It took just one day to get the certificate issued by the court: if a couple applied for a certification of divorce in the morning, they could get the certificate from the court in the afternoon on the same day.[70]

This easy accessibility to consensual divorce, on the one hand, contributed to a speedy settlement of the already broken marriage without unnecessarily causing more pain on the couple or needlessly disclosing private life matters in the process of a divorce law suit, and ensured the couple's "freedom to divorce"; on the other hand, the process was criticized as encouraging a hasty and irresponsible divorce. According to the critics, there were people who would rush to the court in a fit of rage after a trivial domestic dispute without deliberating much on the ramifications of divorce. As a result, the spouses would regret their impulsive actions only after the divorce, realizing that they faced a great loss as the result of the dissolution of their marriage, because they did not consider the issues of child rearing and support payments before ending their marriage. The parties who were obsessed with getting a consensual divorce could not afford to pay enough attention to deciding on a custodian or nurturing parent, or to securing payments of child support expenses.[71] So the provisions for the consensual divorce process were amended in 2007 and the amendment set forth stricter conditions for getting consensual divorce by stipulating a "reflection period" and by requiring an agreement between the spouses on child rearing before the court can give certification of consensual divorce. I will go over briefly below the procedures for consensual divorce and then analyze the role of the family court in determining the child rearing arrangement.

Uniqueness of Consensual Divorce: Agreement on Dissolution of Marriage

For the spouses to obtain consensual divorce in Korea, the spouses need to agree primarily on their intention to divorce and not on divorce arrangements. The couple only needs to agree to dissolve the marriage and on child rearing responsibility, and does not need to agree on the division of marital property or spousal support after divorce. Thus, the Korean consensual divorce is

70 See Jinsu Yune, *supra* note 49, at 249.

71 Jinsu Yune ed., *supra* note 38, at 331.

different from that of France. This comparison needs more explanation of the historical background on the reform of French divorce laws. The first French consensual divorce was prescribed by law of Sept. 20 1792 after the French Revolution and it was possible upon reporting a couple's intention to divorce to the relevant official. Then, the Code Napoleon in 1884 required more stringent requirements such as parents' consent, appearing before the court five times, etc. The Imperial Restoration in 1816 removed consensual divorce from the Code. A complete revision of laws related to divorce in 1975 resurrected consensual divorce,[72] and the French divorce laws were reformed again in 2004.[73] The main differences concerning consensual divorce between the 1975 Code and the 2004 Code are clarification and subdivision of divorce types. "Divorce by acceptance [*le divorce demande acceptée*]" in 1975 which was classified "non-contentious divorce [*le divorce gracieux*]" came to be incorporated into "contentious divorce [*le divorce contentieux*]" in 2004.[74] It makes sense considering the duplicity of "divorce by acceptance": a couple agrees on dissolution of marriage, but they still can have a conflict regarding the arrangements regarding such dissolution. Thus, in order to get "consensual divorce [le divorce par consentement mutuel]," a couple should be in agreement on their intention to divorce as well as the post-divorce arrangements: in France the couple is now required to submit the agreement on all divorce arrangements, including division of property, domicile, support and use of family name after divorce. The Korean consensual divorce is similar to "divorce by acceptance" rather than "consensual divorce" in France. However, an agreement concerning rearing of their children, such as custodianship, visitation rights, and distribution of child support expenses, has been a condition for consensual divorce since 2007 in Korea as we will elaborate later in this article. After the process of confirmation, the parties are required to report their divorce to relevant Korean officers according to "the Act on the Registration, etc. of Family Relationship," in order for the divorce to be valid.

Reflection Period

The reflection period is aimed at preventing hasty divorce. Historically, this sort of waiting period was aggressively implemented for the first time by the

---

72 Loi n 75–617 du 11 juillet 1975 portant réforme du divorce [Law 75–617 of July 11, 1975 for reforming divorce].

73 Loi n 2004–439 du 25 mai 2004 relative au divorce [Law 2004–439 of May 25, 2004 on divorce].

74 Other grounds are 'breakdown divorce [le divorce faillite]' and 'fault divorce [le divorce pour faute].'

Seoul Family Court as an experiment without statutory ground in 2005: a couple who wished to divorce was required to wait a week before they were granted an interview with the judge. It turned out that the rate of withdrawal of the divorce certification applications in this family court rose from eight to nine percent in 2004 and to 16.4 percent in 2005. Furthermore, another aim of the reflection period is to protect minor children and prepare for the situation after divorce. Considerable number of parents rushed into divorce without sufficient deliberation about the negative consequences that a divorce might have on their children. A resolution on issues concerning child-rearing are inevitable in reality even after divorce, but it would be more difficult and burdensome to discuss these issues with ex-spouse after divorce.

Current law provides for two different types of reflection period; one month for a couple with no minor children, and three months for a couple with minor children or yet to be born child. There is an exceptional case in which the court can decide to waive the period when domestic violence or other urgent circumstances are involved.

The pros and cons were considered when introducing the reflection period into the KCC: the negative arguments, mainly made by feminist groups, were that this deliberation period unduly limits the freedom to divorce by wrongly assuming that people who wish to divorce are hasty and imprudent. This could be worth listening to in the sense that it is based on the sort of paternalistic approach of the judiciary. However, the positive argument asserted that if there are even only a few cases of the hasty couples who have wanted immediate divorce but ultimately decide to maintain their marriage after the reflection period, this should be enough reason to keep the reflection period. It is interesting that the French reform of its divorce laws in 2004 abolished the existing reflection period before consensual divorce in order to simplify the procedures.[75]

Agreement on Child-rearing

An agreement between spouses concerning rearing of minor children is a prerequisite for the Korean court's certification of consensual divorce. The agreement needs to address three issues: first, who the custodial parent should be; second, how to distribute the amount of child support payments between the custodial-parent and non-custodial parent; and third, whether to grant the non-custodial parent visitation rights and to what extent.

---

75 Art. 231 de CCF (1975), this article was implemented in 1975 (un delai de reflection de trois mois).

Role of the Family Court

With the consensual divorce reforms, the family court has a considerable role in the consensual divorce process. First, the spouses who wish to divorce by agreement and apply for the confirmation of their mutual intent to divorce must receive the family court's guidance on their divorce. Moreover, the family court, if necessary, may recommend them to get counseling from a professional counselor with the necessary expertise and experience.[76]

Second, the family court has statutory power to make an order to confirm the details of ancillary agreements regarding child-rearing between the divorcing spouses. With respect to the effect of this child support order, a compulsory execution may also be enforced by the court pursuant to this order. This order contains matters related to the determination of the custodian, child support, and visitation rights. If the parties fail to agree on the abovementioned child-rearing matters, the family court may make its determination on such matters. Moreover, the court may change a person with legal and/or physical custody at one party's request or at its discretion.

Assessment

On the one hand, consensual divorce has merit in protecting an innocent spouse. In order to reach an agreement of divorce, an at fault spouse shall consistently persuade the innocent spouse by proposing compensation for pain and suffering damages or paying more for property division. On the other hand, there are couples who manipulate this process of property division for their agenda: a spouse may get consensual divorce falsely in order to evade compulsory execution in favor of creditors, manipulating the consensual divorce process for his/her own purposes. Responding to such manipulation of the consensual divorce process, the courts have ruled in favor of and recognized the exercise of creditor's rights in revoking false consensual divorces.[77]

---

76 For the empirical study of operating counseling system by the Court, see generally Park Bok-Soon, *Hyŏbŭiihonjedoŭi Unyongshilt'ae Mit Kaesŏnbangan* [*The operation and improvement of the system for a divorce by agreement- Focused on the consideration period and counseling recommendation-*], *in* Kajokpŏbyŏn'gu [Korean Journal of Family Law], Vol. 26-1, 11–16 (2012).

77 See Supreme Court [S. Ct.] 2000Da58804, May 8, 2001 (S. Kor.); see also Supreme Court [S. Ct.] 99Da6180, July 28, 2000 (S. Kor.) etc.

III *Judicial Divorce: Grounds for Judicial Divorce*

A Overview

The article 840 of the KCC lists six grounds based on which a judicial divorce can be obtained: (i) if the other spouse has committed an act of unchastity; (ii) if one spouse has been maliciously deserted by the other spouse; (iii) if one spouse has been extremely maltreated by the other spouse or his or her lineal ascendants; (iv) if one spouse's lineal ascendant has been extremely maltreated by the other spouse; (v) if the death or life of the other spouse has been unknown for three years; and (vi) if there exists any other serious cause for making it difficult to continue the marriage. The first five are concrete reasons and the last one is an abstract one. The first two are the so-called common law fault grounds such as unchastity and desertion; the third and fourth reflect the customs and culture of Korea, as they relate to the maltreatment of the spouses as well as of the parents of the spouses. The fifth is unique in the sense that it does not require fault, as it involves the life or death of a spouse being unconfirmed. The last one is general in nature, that is to say, any other serious cause for making it difficult to continue the marriage. The grounds for divorce are the fruit of the mores or the attitudes of the times, and they have to be significant so that there is no room for reconciliation.

This way of mixing the concrete grounds and abstract ground for divorce results in various arguments about the relationship among such grounds.[78] Some explain that each ground is independent, representing a separate cause for judicial divorce, and that one ground does not influence the interpretation of the other grounds. Others regard the concrete grounds in provisions from (i) to (v) as mere illustrative examples, and argue that any one or more of such grounds need to be satisfied, along with the ground (vi) which the only non-illustrative, general condition, in order for judicial divorce to be granted. They further posit that all the grounds should apply to any divorce case and have to be considered together as a whole. The court has ruled that each item is listed as an independent ground, and therefore, that each ground for judicial divorce is a separate condition for a lawsuit.[79] I agree with the former argument, considering that the articles 841 and 842 of KCC provide prescribed periods for

78 Also, there are debates on whether each ground for divorce that is listed in art. 840 of KCC adheres to a fault-based divorce, no-fault divorce, or both. See generally, Dong-Jin Park, *Korean Divorce Law: Can a Spouse Guilty of Marital Misconduct Get a Divorce without the Consent of the Other Spouse?*, *in* International Survey of Family Law 2012, 323–324 (B. Atkin ed., Jordan Publishing Limited, 2012).

79 See Supreme Court [S. Ct.] 62Da812, Jan. 31, 1963 (S. Kor.); Supreme Court [S. Ct.] 99Meu1886, Sept. 5, 2000 (S. Kor.).

effectiveness regarding the grounds (i) and (vi) respectively. The court should judge only the ground the petitioning party is claiming and the other items should be separate.

B Grounds for Judicial Divorce

Unchastity

Adultery is a typical ground for divorce from historical and comparative legal approach. However, the Korean Civil Code stipulates "unchastity" rather than "adultery" as a cause for divorce. Unchastity is a wider concept that covers adultery, so in the case of a man and a woman who were found wearing only underwear in a hotel room, even though their adultery was not proved, the court recognized that there was unchasity.[80] If a spouse has committed an act of unchastity voluntarily during a marriage, the other spouse can apply for a divorce suit.

The unfaithful spouse, however, could raise the following defenses in the divorce suit: the claimant spouse gave a prior consent or an *ex post facto* tolerance, or a considerable time passed after the act of unchastity (art. 841 of KCC). First, the prior consent could be given in an express or implied way, and if the defendant spouse succeeds in proving the existence of the prior consent, the divorce suit shall be dismissed. Next, an *ex post facto* tolerance should be expressed voluntarily after a spouse had certainly recognized the other spouse's unchastity, and nonetheless a true intent to continue the marriage relationship should be represented in clear and reliable way. Lastly, if six months have passed since the spouse became aware of such act of unchastity of the other spouse, or if two years have passed since the occurrence of such event, the spouse may not file for divorce with the court.

So far, verifying adultery in a divorce law suit has not been an issue in Korea, because generally the claimant spouse filing for divorce on the ground of adultery simultaneously accuses the other spouse of adultery under criminal law as well. Then, the police and prosecutor investigate and collect evidence of an extramarital affair to prove guilt and the claimant spouse can use the evidence gathered from this criminal investigation in its divorce lawsuit against the other spouse. However, adultery is no longer a criminal offense in Korea, as the Constitution Court of Korea ruled on Feb. 26, 2015 that the anti-adultery

80 See Supreme Court [S. Ct.] 87Meu5, Mai 6, 1987 (S. Kor.). For the case where a wife lives together with a man who has copulative impotence due to stroke, the court recognized her unchastity, see Supreme Court [S. Ct.] 92Meu68, Nov. 10, 1992 (S. Kor.).

provision, article 241 of the Criminal Act,[81] is unconstitutional.[82] This provision imposes imprisonment of less than two years as the only statutory sentence in the criminal punishment of adultery or fornication with a married person.[83]

In this seven-to-two decision, the majority opinion ruled that making adultery a criminal offense is unconstitutional in that it infringes on sexual autonomy and privacy of an individual. Its arguments are as follows: as social structure and people's recognition of sex have changed, the public's view of the individual rights to sexual autonomy is evolving; thus, it is not appropriate to bring criminal charges against all acts that some may find morally reprehensible. Further, criminal punishments of adultery or fornication are not actually effective in promoting monogamy and protecting families. The duty of faithfulness between couples and protection of women could be achieved effectively by granting of judicial divorce and damages against the unfaithful spouse. The minority opinion argued, to the contrary, that the view that adultery harms social order and violates other's right is still valid, and the right to commit adultery is not part of the individual rights protected by the Constitution, in that it destroys a marriage system based on monogamy and has a devastating impact on maintaining and protecting the family unit.

As adultery is no longer a criminal offence, proving adultery is now more burdensome to the claimant spouse filing for divorce based on the adultery ground, and the claimant may now have to employ a private detective to run a careful and secret investigation and collect evidence.

Malevolent Desertion

When one spouse maliciously deserts the other spouse, it falls under the ground for divorce pursuant to article 840 Item 2 of KCC. One spouse must desert the other spouse and the desertion must result from his or her malice, and

81 *Hyongbeob* [Criminal Act], Act. No. 293, Sept. 18, 1953, art. 241 (S. Kor.) (Adultery) (1) A married person who commits adultery shall be punished by imprisonment for not more than two years. The same shall apply to the other participant. (2) The crime in the preceding paragraph shall be prosecuted only upon the complaint of the victimized spouse. If the victimized spouse condones or pardons the adultery, complaint can no longer be made.

82 Constitutional Court [Const. Ct], 2009Hun-ba17·205, 2010Hun-ba194, 2011Hun-ba 4, 2012Hun-ba 57·255·411, 2013Hun-ba139·161·267·342·365, 2014Hun-ba53·464, 2011Hun-ka31, 2014Hun-ka4 (Consolidated). Feb. 26, 2015 (S. Kor.).

83 Interestingly, the Court previously ruled this article constitutional four times on September 10, 1990, March 11, 1993, October 25, 2001 and October 30, 2008 respectively 89Hun-Ma82, 90Hun-Ka70, 2000Hun-ba60, and 2007Hun-ka17·221, 2008Hun-ka7·26, 2008Hun-ba21·47 (Consolidated).

there must be no reasonable cause. This is a typical ground for divorce found in divorce laws of other nations.[84] A desertion here means abolition of marital cohabitation, violating the duty of living together, a basic element of marriage. Though the law does not require expressly, the abolition of marital cohabitation should last for a considerable period. Malice is the intent to desert his or her spouse permanently, and a concept containing reprehensible ethical element. If one spouse happened to separate unavoidably due to job, medical treatment, or imprisonment, there exists a reasonable cause to violate the duty of living together. This ground has dual nature: it is a fault based ground, in that it requires intentional violation of the duty of cohabitation; while it is a no-fault ground, in that extensive time away from each other for unavoidable reasons may be deemed to violate the duty of the spouses to live together.

Maltreatment of or to Other Spouse or Lineal Ascendants

If one spouse has been extremely maltreated by the other spouse or his or her lineal ascendants (art. 840 Item 3 of KCC) or if one spouse's lineal ascendant has been extremely maltreated by the other spouse (art. 840 Item 4 of KCC), the spouse may file for divorce. One spouse's maltreatment by the other spouse is a typical ground found in laws of other jurisdictions,[85] but maltreatment of ascendants of one spouse by the other spouse or maltreatment of one spouse by ascendants of the other spouse are unique from a comparative law perspective. These provisions were first implemented as a result of the similar Japanese law that applied to the Korean people during the Japanese colonial period and of the traditional Korean customs having roots in Chosŏn Dynasty. Japan revoked the law that was a predecessor to this Korean law in 1947. And although the long-held custom of honoring extended families was prevalent at the time of the enactment of the KCC, as the age of a nuclear family has arrived in Korea, a doubt is raised about the need of these provisions. According to critics of these provisions, they are a relic of the past and do not harmonize with the present nuclear family model. So they should be abolished from the KCC, and they should be absorbed into the general ground of (vi). This opinion is persuasive and is worthy of attention. Another critique is that there is no designated period of effectiveness for these provisions.

---

84 For example, *Bürgerliches Gesetzbuch* [BGB] [German Civil Code], Aug. 18, 1896, § 1567 (it was deleted by Marriage Act of 1938); Code Civil [CC] Dec.10, 1907, SR 210, art. 140 (Switz.) (it was deleted in 1999 reform); Minpo (Civ. C.) art. 770 (2) (Japan) etc.

85 For example, Code Civil [C.civ] art. 231 (Fr.) (it was deleted in 1974 reform); Code Civil [CC] Dec.10, 1907, SR 210, art. 138 (Switz.) (it was deleted in 1999 reform); Minpo (Civ. C.) art. 813 (Japan) (it was deleted in 1947 reform) etc.

In practice, extreme maltreatment may be defined as cruelty or grave insult that gives rise to a reasonable comprehension of danger. It is a conduct that adversely affects physical or mental health of one spouse, and such a conduct leads to unbearable pain for the spouse when the spouse is forced to continue with such marital life. The court shall judge whether an act is an extreme maltreatment to permit a divorce, based on a comprehensive consideration of various circumstances of the marital relationship including the age, educational background, and job of the parties, the motivation, manner, result of an act, the duration of marriage, whether there is minor children between the couples. For example, in the case where a father-in-law verbally abuses a daughter-in-law habitually, yelling her to go back to her parents' home whenever he drinks, the court has recognized that she is extremely maltreated by the other spouse's lineal ascendants.[86]

Death or Life of One Spouse Has Been Unknown

Only if the death or life of one spouse has been unknown for three years, then the other spouse may seek divorce. It is rare from the comparative law perspective. That the death or life of a spouse has been unknown means the state in which neither the spouse's survival nor passing can be proved. This is a no-fault divorce ground in that the cause, reason, whether there is fault or not shall not be considered. If it is uncertain for five years whether a spouse is alive or dead, then a Judicial Declaration of Disappearance may be made.[87] However, this ground for divorce is different from Judicial Declaration of Disappearance, in which the distribution of inheritance is commenced, but if the Declaration is annulled, the marriage would be revived. There is no prescribed period of effectiveness for this ground.

Abstract Grounds: Other Serious Causes

The abstract or general ground for judicial divorce, "there is a serious reason that makes it difficult to continue the marriage," is stipulated in Article 840 subparagraph 6 of KCC.

There have been opposing arguments over the interpretation of this provision. The court's ruling requires two elements: an objective one as well a subjective one. First, the marital relationship between the spouses should be such that it is impossible to restore, and the marital relationship corresponds to the essence of marriage based upon love and trust between husband and

---

86 Supreme Court [S. Ct.] 68Meu29, March 25, 1969 (S. Kor.).

87 Art. 27 of KCC.

wife. Second, it should be an unbearable pain for the spouse to be forced to continue such marital life.[88]

This ground covers incurable mental illness,[89] psychiatric disorders, drug addiction, gambling addiction, religious conflict, criminal activity by a spouse, imprisonment, long-term separation, and extremely patriarchal attitudes. However, neither a wife's infertility nor a husband's impotence by aspermia is covered under this ground for divorce.[90]

There is a prescribed period of effectiveness for this ground: if six months have passed since the spouse was aware of such ground, or if two years have passed since the happening of such ground, the spouse may not apply to the court for divorce.[91] However, considering this is a ground based on no-fault or irretrievable breakdown, it is hard to understand prescribing a period of effectiveness for this ground. Thus, it appears that such prescribed period is without merit and represents legislative error.[92]

IV *Judicial Divorce: Fault Based and No-fault Divorce*

A Controversy

The argument concerning fault-based divorce or no-fault divorce has been a long debated topic in discussions about Korean divorce laws.[93] The arguments echo those in the western countries. The pros and cons have been exhaustively debated both in the popular press and in the academic community, especially before the en banc decision concerning this issue was rendered.

In a recent en banc decision on September 15, 2015,[94] the Supreme Court affirmed the preexisting case law that does not allow a family court to grant a judicial divorce in response to a petition by an at-fault spouse. In this case, the claimant "A," got married to "B" in 1976 but had a love child with "C" in 1998. A left B in 2001 and he cohabited with C until he filed for divorce against B in 2011. The defendant B is a 65 year old woman plagued with illness and she refuses to divorce. B had raised their three children by herself after A left them, providing them only with 1,000,000 KW (900 USD) per month. A needs his cohabitant C's

88 Supreme Court [S. Ct.] 2005Meu1689, Dec. 23, 2005 (S. Kor.).

89 Supreme Court [S. Ct.] 90Meu446, Jan. 15, 1991 (S. Kor.); Supreme Court [S. Ct.] 91Meu627, Dec. 24, 1991 (S. Kor.).

90 Supreme Court [S. Ct.] 65Meu37, Sept. 21, 1965 (S. Kor.); Supreme Court [S. Ct.] 82Meu36, Nov. 23, 1982 (S. Kor.).

91 Art. 842 of KCC.

92 Yune Jinsu ed., *supra* note 38, at 473.

93 A detailed discussion of this is beyond the scope of this article, but see generally Dong-Jin Park, *supra* note 78, at 324–325.

94 Supreme Court [S. Ct.], 2013Meu568, Sept. 15, 2015 (S. Kor.).

care because of diabetes. He once asked his wife and grown-up children to be a kidney donor for him in late 2011, only to be refused. Also, A and C's daughter is a minor needing parental care.

In this seven-to-six decision, the majority opinion argued as follows: first, the door is left open for even an at-fault spouse to part with the other spouse through the consensual divorce system that is unique in Korea. The at-fault spouse should have persuaded the other spouse with sincerity and sufficient compensation. Second, a ruling in favor of judicial divorce could put the innocent spouse at risk, due to the absence of hardship clause and systems that financially protect the spouse and children under the present law. The innocent spouse cannot help but bear a considerable risk that might unilaterally be sacrificed for the at-fault spouse's happiness, if the spouse's divorce claim were to be broadly recognized by taking a no-fault divorce approach. Third, the Court ruled that considering that most part of fault would be having an affair, but as adultery could not be punished by the Korean Criminal Code any more,[95] a favorable ruling could result in a risk of admitting bigamy that the Civil Code does not allow.[96, 97] Instituting penal provisions on bigamy in exchange for abolishing adultery must take precedence. Last but not least, the reality that the status of women is inferior to those of men in the Korean society should not be overlooked. Korea still has a long way to go to realize a genuine gender equality in socio-economic arena, including employment, wage, and childcare. Nor did the court thought that it could turn a blind eye to those cases where the no-fault spouse suffers from a severe emotional distress and destitution by the at-fault spouse's divorce claim.

Meanwhile, the dissenting opinion pointed that the changes in the general perception of divorce in the society at large and in law and practice on divorce, lowers the necessity to restrict interpretation of Item 6 of KCC. As long

---

95 Constitutional Court [Const. Ct.], 2009Hun-ba17·20 et al., Fev. 26, 2015 (S. Kor.). In this case, the Constitutional Court decided that art. 241 of Criminal Act, which imposes imprisonment as the only statutory sentence in the criminal punishment of adultery or fornication with a married person, is unconstitutional.

96 Art. 810 of KCC (Prohibition of Bigamy) No one who has a spouse shall enter into another marriage.
Art. 818 of KCC (Claimant for Annulment of Bigamy) In the case of marriage in violation of the provisions of art. 810, a claim for annulment of the marriage to the court may be made by either party, the spouse, the lineal ascendants, the collateral blood relatives within the fourth degree of relationship, or a public prosecutor.

97 However, this reason does not seem to be logical, in that as long as 'bigamy' means an act of entering a marriage with one person while still legally married to another person, admitting no fault divorce may not cause bigamy.

as the communal married life relationship is objectively found to have irretrievably broken down, it would be reasonable to conclusively grant a claim for divorce to dissolve the marital relationship that is a mere formality, even though the other spouse has an intention to continue the marriage. It pointed out the potential for greater pain and hardship involving the process of proving the other spouse's fault in the divorce law suit. Then, it insisted that balance and harmony should be struck between the liability attributed to the spouse claiming for divorce and the protection and consideration for the other spouse: by sufficiently reflecting the liability of the at-fault spouse when setting the amount of damages for emotional distress due to the breakdown of marriage, thereby allowing for substantial compensation for the other spouse; and by amply considering the spousal support elements, as well as liquidating the property relation formed during marriage. When estimating the proportion and amount of property division, thereby ensuring the other spouse's livelihood would be as secured after divorce as in marriage. Furthermore, it specified the exceptions for granting the at-fault spouse's claim for divorce in instances that would be manifestly contrary to a sense of justice and fairness and cause a serious harm to the interests of the other spouse or child: where a divorce would put the non-liable spouse in a severely harsh emotional, social, and economic situation; where the parents' divorce would seriously harm the support, education, and best interests of the child; where at-fault spouse has intentionally forsaken the spousal and child support obligations over an extended period during the marriage; and where the spouse may, in the Court's opinion, drive the other spouse into destitution by deliberately evading the performance of property distribution and damages payment.

I agree with the majority opinion, in that the freedom to divorce could be guaranteed by consensual divorce, and that protecting the intent of non-responsible party to keep the marriage even though broken. There must be reasons that the innocent spouse would deny a divorce even though the couple has not lived together for a long time, that is to say, the marriage broke down irreparably in terms of the couple's cohabitation relation. Whether it is a financial concern after the divorce, a parent's concern for his/her child, or a strong feeling against becoming a divorcee, such private reasons should not be overlooked. That is because these reasons reflect desperate situations for the innocent spouse, taking into account the stark realities of social disadvantage towards the divorcee or children of the divorced family.

Therefore, when there is a irretrievable breakdown of marriage, the family court should be prudent with wisdom of Solomon in exercising the power and discretion. In this way the definition of marriage and general contract theory need to be revisited. Marriage is a contract formally entered into between a man and a woman of marriageable age. A contract is binding between the parties: *Pacta sunt servanda.* The parties at fault in non-performance cannot revoke the contract unilaterally. The resolution of "change in circumstances" (*clausula rebus sic stantibus*) is permitted quite exceptionally. At least, these basic concepts should be maintained in a contract of marriage. If one spouse commits a fault or there is an irretrievable breakdown, non-responsible spouse can seek a judicial divorce against the at fault spouse. However, there are special circumstances where there is not so much marriage-breakdown liability left as to reject a divorce claim, then the court may grant the reliable party a judicial divorce exceptionally. Let's see the case law accumulated.

B Case Law

General Principle

In principle, a spouse who is mainly responsible for the failure of the marital life may not claim divorce on the ground of such failure in Korea. Even though the at-fault spouse proves that there is an irreconcilable difference between the couple, the court would not grant divorce. Whether the courts permit the at-fault spouse's petition for divorce is a matter of legislative policy. Even though there is no provision that limits a claimant for divorce suit to be an innocent spouse, the courts have consistently ruled that only an innocent spouse could petition for divorce since 1965.[98]

Exceptional Circumstances

However, the courts' rulings made exceptions to the steadfast rule in several decisions in the late 1980's: divorce claims by the responsible spouse may be granted as an exception when there are special circumstances.[99] First, when the other spouse is not accepting the divorce claim out of obstinacy or retaliatory sentiment, or is bringing a counteraction, while it is objectively obvious that the latter has no intent to continue to be married after the failure of marriage,[100] there is no concern for a divorce to expel the other spouse by one spouse's unilateral intent. Second, when the spouse's fault happened after a marriage had broken down, there is no cause-and-effect relationship between fault and breakdown.[101] Third, it is when the liability of the spouse allegedly

---

98 Supreme Court [S. Ct.] 65Meu37, Sept. 21, 1965 (S. Kor.).

99 For the analysis of the exceptional cases granting a divorce to the at-fault spouse according to circumstances, see Dong-Jin Park, *supra* note 78, at 328–334.

100 Supreme Court [S. Ct.] 86Meu28, Apr. 14, 1987 (S. Kor.); Supreme Court [S. Ct.] 2004Meu1378, Jan. 13, 2006 (S. Kor.)

101 Supreme Court [S. Ct.] 87Meu9, Apr. 25, 1988 (S. Kor.).

at fault as to the breakdown of marital relation does not outweigh that of the other spouse.[102]

The purpose of prohibiting a divorce claim by an at-fault spouse is to prevent an outcome contrary to the morality demanded by the institution of marriage or the principle of good faith. In cases where an at-fault spouse's liability is not so much as to reject his/her divorce claim, such spouse's divorce claim may be granted so long as it does not raise concerns for destroying the institutions of marriage and family and is not contrary to the morality and ethics of society.[103]

In determining whether to grant an at-fault spouse's divorce claim as an exception, the Court should take various circumstances of the marital relationship in account: these circumstances include the type and extent of the at-fault spouse's liability, the other spouse's intention to remain in the marriage and sentiment towards the at-fault spouse, the age of the parties, the duration of marriage, the specific lifestyle during marriage, the duration of separation, the lifestyle formed after the couple's separation, whether there was any change in circumstances after the marriage breakdown, the anticipated emotional, social, and economic situation and the level of social security of the other spouse in case a divorce were to be granted, and the support, education, and best interests of any minor child.

The exception should be admitted very limitedly and the non-reliable party's intent, protection and distress should be considered mainly: where there is no concern to expel the non-responsible spouse unilaterally because the non-responsible spouse does not intend to remain in the marriage; where the protection and consideration of the non-responsible spouse and children are amply provided to the point of offsetting the liability of the claimant spouse; where the passage of time has reached to render it meaningless to scrutinize the relative liabilities of both parties any more, with the diminution of both the at-fault spouse's liability which was once manifest at the time of the marriage breakdown and the emotional distress on the part of the non-responsible spouse.[104]

---

102 See Supreme Court [S. Ct.] 88Meu740, June 27, 1989 (S. Kor.); Supreme Court [S. Ct.] 90Meu552, Jan. 11, 1991 (S. Kor.).

103 Supreme Court [S. Ct.] en banc decision 2013Meu568, Sept. 15, 2015 (S. Kor.).

104 Supreme Court 2009Meu2130 Dec. 24, 2009 (S. Kor.) holds that:

...As dissolution status of marital cohabitation relation between the plaintiff and the defendant becomes prolonged, the plaintiff's liability considerably weakened as time goes by, and in light of the plaintiff's circumstance, its social acknowledgment and legal assessment cannot avoid being modified. Under the current circumstance, a strict analysis

V *Conclusions*

According to a standard which classifies divorce laws of a country into five steps or stages,[105] the level of Korean divorce laws is still at the first stage at most: it "accepts breakdown of the marriage as ground for divorce, alongside different forms of 'fault' by one spouse." Then, is Korean divorce laws undeveloped or left behind, because it still sticks to fault-based divorce policy? Based on the assumption that the freedom to divorce is not the only value to uphold, I do not agree that the marriage or family already broken or without love does not need to be protected. One spouse's desire to keep the marriage as well as the other spouse's desire to dissolute marriage should be considered.[106] In the same sense, I cannot agree with the argument for the fifth stage that "the law should contain only one single ground for divorce, and that the desire of a spouse to terminate the marriage should be respected." This argument leaves open the question as to whether one's desire to end the marriage should be upheld more than the other's desire to keep the marriage. The grounds

---

of degree of liability as criterion for deciding the plaintiff and the defendant's divorce does no longer have any legal and social meaning, and determination of the weight of both sides' liability itself came to a difficult situation. The defendant just wants to continue a superficial legal marriage relation, which lacks in the substance of marriage. If the current dire circumstance continues pursuant to the defendant's intent to continue marriage, it would bring unendurable suffering especially to the plaintiff.

In light of other circumstances relied on by the court below, the plaintiff and the defendant's marriage broke down irreparably in terms of couple cohabitation relation, which is an essential aspect of marital relation. To enforce continuation of marital life constitutes an unendurable suffering for one spouse. In light of purpose of the institution of marriage and the principle of good faith as the leading principle of the Civil Code, the plaintiff's liability as to the breakdown of marriage relation is not so serious enough to reject the plaintiff's claim for divorce.

105 Anders Agell, *Grounds and Procedures Reviewed, in* Economic Consequences of Divorce: The International Perspective 54–55 (Weitzman & Maclean eds., 1992). A second Step is to accept breakdown of the marriage as the only ground for divorce; a third one is to make less stringent requirement for proving irretrievable and permanent breakdown of marital relation; a fourth one is to accept unilateral divorce meaning that a spouse's application is sufficient; a fifth one is to accept unilateral divorce in more liberal sense that a spouse's desire to dissolute marriage shall be respected itself. Agell expects that most industrialized countries will keep developing its legislation continuously until they reach stage 4 or stage 5.

106 Park Bok-Soon & Lee Yeo-Bong, *Ŭishikchosarŭl T'onghan P'at'anjuŭi Toip Kanŭngsŏng Mosaek* [*Exploration of the Possibility of Acceptance Breakdown Divorce Priciole through Surveys of Perceptions*], *in* Kajokpŏbyŏn'gu [Korean Journal of Family Law], Vol. 27-1, 333 (2013).

should not be a subjective desire of the parties nor an objective irretrievableness, rather they should address whether there remains anything worth protecting in their marriage.

As reviewed earlier in this chapter, the freedom to divorce is guaranteed by the system of consensual divorce in Korea. The risk of abusing easy accessibility to consensual divorce could be hedged through reflection period and the family court's intervention on child rearing in the process for the consensual divorce.

The controversial issue concerning fault-based or no-fault divorce has been settled for the time being by the en banc decision mentioned above. Furthermore, this decision will cause to postpone the introduction of no-fault divorce law in Korea for many years until the Court overrules this decision. However, as the decision was split 7 to 6, the chance to conflict in the future is still left. A magazine article titled "A time-limited fault-based divorce law which is standing in the way of no-fault divorce law,"[107] which elaborated on this decision, reflected the widely held view that Korea is moving towards no-fault divorce. Two women Justices on the Court took different positions on this decision. It is not a coincidence that the only divorced Justice, Park Bo-young, sided with the majority opinion. She stressed out the vulnerable status of the divorced women and children after divorce. In the next two chapters, we look into the Korean present situation in the economic consequences of divorce on couples and on child.

Part IV Marital Property Settlement upon Divorce

I *Overview*

Issues of the economic consequences, such as the division of marital property, the nature of marital property, and the purpose and length of spousal support upon dissolution, have been still focused on during the divorce process, even though Korean law has kept the "fault-based divorce" principle. A concern of protecting the divorced economically after divorce does not follow as a logical consequence of introducing "no-fault divorce"; rather it is subsequent to the development of an awareness in the matrimonial litigation. The warning or worries in western countries must have been a salutary lesson for Korea.[108] Under the "fault-based divorce" principle in Korea, the claimant has two

107 http://h21.hani.co.kr/arti/society/society_general/40395.html (Sept. 23, 2015 *Hangyeorye 21*).

108 See generally Weitzman, *supra* note 14, 323 ff. For critiques on Weitzman's findings, see Hoffman, Saul & Duncan Greg, *supra* note 16, at 641–645; see also Peterson,

rights: the one is a right to demand liquidation of the marital property upon divorce; the other is the damages against a liable spouse for the cause of divorce.[109] The former is a claim for property division, while the latter is a claim for pain and suffering damages.

A claim for damages, especially compensation for psychiatric harm, performed the only and primary function as an economic consequence of divorce before the reform in 1990. However, a claim for damages requires proving the other spouse's fault, so it is limited in scope and there were criticisms that liquidation on divorce or support after divorce through damages is neither a normal nor a reasonable operation. Thus, the claim for property division was introduced in the KCC in 1990.

Under the community system such as French Civil Code (art. 1441ff), some states in USA), it is necessary to grant claims for property division, while under separate systems such as German Civil Code (§1363), Swiss Civil Code (§§ 204ff), Japanese Civil Code (art. 762), or some states in USA, it is widely accepted.

Unlike several countries' Civil Codes approving a duty of support between couple after divorce, such as French Civil Code (art. 270ff), German Civil Code (§§1570ff), Swiss Civil Code (§§125ff), or some states in the USA, the KCC does not recognize any support after divorce or alimony.

II *Management of Marital Property*

According to freedom of contract principles, would-be husband and wife can make a contract on their property relation between them after marriage. However, not all couples decide on management of marital property before marriage; thus the KCC provides a separate system which consists of peculiar property and assumed community property.

A Premarital Contracts

A man and a woman who are going to get married can enter into a contract with respect to their marital property (art. 829 (1)). They should conclude a contract prior to marriage, and once the contract is finalized, they cannot change it during marriage without the Court's permission based on a justifiable reason. There is no restriction on the form of the contract, but the registration is required for setting up against third parties (art. 829 (5)). In practice, however, this antenuptial agreement is nominal, and very few couples seem to use it.

Richard R., *supra* note 16, at 528–536. For Weitzman's response to critiques, see Lenore J. Weitzman, *supra* note 16, at 528–536, *supra* note 16, at 537–538, *supra* note 14.

109 Jinsu Yune ed., *supra* note 38, at 371.

B Legal Marital Property System: Separate Property System

In the absence of premarital agreement, which specifies property management responsibilities, all marital property relation shall be governed by the provision of the KCC (art. 829 (1)), basically a separate system.[110] First, the inherent property acquired prior to the marriage, and any property acquired by one spouse during the marriage in his or her own title through gift, devise, or bequest is peculiar property (art. 830 (1)). Second, any property, of which title is uncertain between the husband and wife, shall be presumed to be in their co-ownership (art. 830 (2)). Husband or wife shall separately manage, use and take profit from his or her peculiar property (art. 831).

III *Division of Marital Property*

A Purpose of Property Division

A separate property system has a defect that the full-time housewife usually has hardship after divorce under the practice where most property acquired by common efforts during marriage is acquired under the husband's title, if he is the only bread-winner. So property division system was adopted to improve and solve issues concerning this defect. The property division system divides each spouse's portion upon divorce based on substance, not on title, regarding assets accumulated on co-living. It aims at guaranteeing freedom of divorce practically and realizing gender-equality.[111] As to property acquired by common efforts, the wife's indirect contribution of domestic labor as well as direct contribution to the family income should be considered. The wife's giving up her opportunity in economic activity in order to concentrate on child-rearing needs to be considered and compensated. The claim for property division shall be extinguished after two years have passed from the date of divorce.

B Contents of Claims for Property Division

Three elements could be considered as main criteria of property division: liquidation, support and consolation. The prevalent decisions ruled that property division system mainly aims at liquidation and distribution of common property actually acquired during marriage.[112] Some decisions ruled that support after divorce as well as liquidation of marital property shall be considered

---

110 See Kim Joo-soo & Kim Sang-yong, *supra* note 39, at 136: see also Jin-su Yune ed., *supra* note 38, at 267.

111 Supreme Court [S. Ct.], en banc Decision 2010Meu4071, June 20, 2013 (S. Kor.).

112 See Supreme Court [S. Ct.] 93Seu6, May, 11, 1993 (S. Kor.); Supreme Court [S. Ct.] 95Meu175, Sept. 12, 1995 (S. Kor.); Supreme Court [S. Ct.] 98Meu1486, Feb. 13, 1998 (S. Kor.); Supreme Court [S. Ct.], en banc Decision 2012Meu2888, July 16, 2014 (S. Kor.).

in a property division claim.[113] Other decisions included damages for mental suffering as property division's nature.[114]

As long as the couple has property attained by both parties' cooperation at judgment of divorce, the family court shall determine the amount and method of division upon the party's claim in light of both parties' whole circumstances such as their respective contribution to obtaining the property. First, the court will go through a process to classify which property and debt is to be considered marital. Next, it will assign a monetary value on the marital property and debt. Lastly, it will distribute the marital assets between the two parties in an equitable way. The existence and value of property as object of division requires strict proof, while the ratio of division is left to the judge's discretion.

C Scope of Property as Object of Division

General Criteria

The KCC provides that "a party to divorce can claim property division to the other" and "the family court decides amount and method on the party's claim in consideration of property formed by couple's cooperation amount and other factors (art. 839-2(1) and (2))".

If claims for marital property division are filed, the family court has to begin the process by classifying property accumulated during the marriage into two categories: one would be separate property; the other would be marital property. The court allows each party to keep his or her separate property and then divides the marital property. The property acquired before the marriage, any property acquired by bequest, devise, descent during marriage, any gifts to one spouse from anyone other than the other spouse, any separate property acquired in exchange for separate property are separate property. The property whose title is under the name of one of the parties is presumptively the property of that party.

If the spouse contributed actively to maintain or to augment the other spouse's peculiar property, this property shall be an object of property division. For example, if one spouse took an active part in trading in real estate, which other spouse had acquired through devise before marriage and the value of this peculiar property increased, the other spouse's contribution should be reimbursed by dividing this property upon divorce. The court uses equitable factors in the distribution of marital property. As to the scope of marital property as object of division, there has been much development in the rulings that

113 Supreme Court [S. Ct.], en banc Decision 2010Meu4071, 4088, June 20, 2013 (S. Kor.).

114 See Supreme Court [S. Ct.] 2005Da73105, June 29, 2006 (S. Kor.), etc.

specify such scope of marital property; however, there is still room for interpretation in determining such scope.

Marital Debt

Should marital debts, like marital property, be divided equally between spouses or apportioned equitably? The issue of marital debt is a little different than that of marital property. The first issue here for the court to decide is the criteria for dividing marital debt and separate debt: If a debt is incurred jointly, then a presumption arises that it is a marital debt; if a debt is incurred separately, then a presumption arises that it is a separate debt. After considering the joint signatures of the parties, the nature of the item purchased, or any circumstance that evidences the couple's intent, if the court determines that one spouse's debt to a third party is indeed incurred by the couple's common property formation or securing family living expenses, then this debt is divided between them.[115]

The second issue is whether property division claim can be accepted, where the couple's total negative property at divorce exceeds their total positive property which results in debt division during the process of property division. In a recent en bans decision dated June 20, 2013, the Korean Supreme Court addressed the division of property for a couple with more debt than assets.[116] In this eight-to-five decision, the majority opinion overruled the preexisting case law, which held the other's property division claim is rejected where one spouse has debt and nothing left when the debt is deducted from total property.[117] Its argument are as follows: divisible property is not limited to positive property according to article 839 of the KCC; if the property division system divides each spouse's portion of acquired assets based on substance, not title, at time of divorce, and takes into account co-living and common debt, it is fair to both consider positive property and negative property in determining property division arrangements. Therefore, in case of the debt exceeding the total assets or the decrease in the total assets by common debt, the total circumstances shall be considered such as debt incurrence, use, contents, amount, marital life, economic activity ability, future prospect, and its division method. In other words, negative property division is unlike positive property division where uniform rate is applied depending on contribution to property.

---

115 Supreme Court [S. Ct.] 92Meu501, May 25, 1993 (S. Kor.), etc.

116 Supreme Court en banc Decision 2010Meu4071,4088, June 20, 2013 (S. Kor.).

117 See Supreme Court [S. Ct.] 97Meu933, Sept. 26, 1997 (S. Kor.); Supreme Court [S. Ct.] 2001Meu718, Sept. 4, 2002 (S. Kor.) etc.

In property division claim, liquidation of property acquired in marriage and support after divorce shall be considered.

National Pension

All the citizens whose age is between eighteen and sixty, residing in the Republic of Korea, shall be insured under the National Pension Scheme since 1999 (art. 6 of the National Pension Act). Before then, a subscription was optional. The national pension is one of the social insurances based on social solidarity for the purpose of insuring the stable livelihood and welfare for old-age or death: it functions as intergenerational and intra-generational redistribution. Public officials, military personnel and private school teachers and staff to whom the Public Officials Pension Act, the Military Pension Act and the Pension for Private School Teachers and Staff Act apply are not national pension subscribers as we discuss right behind.

Regarding the national pension, there is an issue whether a former spouse of an insured person should take a lump-sum payment on divorce or take a pay-as-you-go payment whenever the insured spouse become old-age beneficiary. The court could have power to grant two kinds of orders in relation to pension: pension attachment order and pension sharing order; the former is an order of the court to earmark some of a spouse's future pension in favor of the other on condition that a pensioner survives; the latter is a better solution in that it re-adjusts the spouses' pension entitlements and enables each party to make future pension independently of the other.

The provision of article 64 of the National Pension Act chooses the latter, providing that the divorced spouse's national pension accumulated during the period of marriage of over five years is divided in half.[118] Once a spouse over sixty years old shall claim division of national pension within three years from the time when the former spouse become an old-age pensioner, the pension should be divided. Or, in case when a spouse gets a divorce before sixty years old, the spouse can claim the pension division in advance within three years from the effective date of the divorce. Then, the pension shall be divided when the former spouse become an old-age pensioner.[119] Some critics point out the way to divide equally and uniformly the accumulated pension during the period of marriage over five years is not reasonable.

---

118 *Kungminyŏn'gŭmbŏp* [National Pension Act], Act No. 8541, July 23, 2007.7.23, art. 64 (S. Kor.).

119 *Kungminyŏn'gŭmbŏp* [National Pension Act], Act No. 13642, Dec. 29, 2015.7.23, art. 64-3 (S. Kor.). This newly added provision will take effect on Dec. 30, 2016.

Retirement Pension Benefits

Retirement pension benefits are increasingly becoming bigger part of financial assets, and comprise a large proportion of marital property these days. The following issues arise: whether non-vested pension could be divided upon divorce; when should the retirement or pension benefits be divided by the annuity method; whether its division proportion could be decided individually and differently from other general properties as a whole in view of all circumstances considered in property division. The retirement pension subscribers here mean the public officials, the private school teachers and staff, and the military pension whom the Public Officials Pension Act, the Military Pension Act and the Pension for Private School Teachers and Staff Act apply, because all other citizen are insured under the national pension as mentioned earlier.

When one of the parties actually receives his or her retirement pension upon divorce, that-is-to-say on the date of closing fact-finding proceedings at the trial court, the above retirement pension is inseparable mixture of social security and late wage payment; as long as the other spouse's cooperation during the period of marriage is recognized, a portion of the above retirement pension entitlement pertinent to that period can be seen as property achieved by both parties' cooperation.[120] Thus already vested retirement pension entitlement is subject to property division like general properties.

Even though one of the parties is still working at the time of the divorce and a retirement pension is not yet vested, the right of claim for retirement pension should be an object of property division. The rationale is almost the same as already vested retirement pension for the reason that pension benefits are like deferred compensation, and therefore the non-employee spouse has an interest in that pension benefit upon divorce. If this interest can be valued, it should be divisible upon divorce, even though it vests in the future. In a recent en banc decision dated July 16, 2014, the majority opinion of the Korean Supreme Court overruled the preexisting case law, which excluded a public official's retirement pension entitlement from an object of property division and rather took it into account as mere "other circumstance" for evaluating contents and method of property division, for the reason that retirement pension recipient spouse's remaining life span cannot be confirmed. Its argument are as follows: it would trigger a grossly unfair result compared to where the spouse receives retirement payout not as annuity but as a lump sum payment; as the degree of taking "other circumstance" into account is not based on a clear criterion; it would be in line with article 64 of the National Pension Act providing that the divorced spouse's national pension accumulated during the marriage period of

120 Supreme Court Decision [S. Ct.] 95Nu7529, Sep. 29, 1995 (S. Kor.).

over five years shall be divided in half. Retirement pension entitlement exists already potentially and real evaluation of its economic value is possible on the date of closing for the fact-finding proceedings at a trial court. Specifically, the amount will be the equivalent of retirement pension entitlement the spouse will receive if employee spouse retires upon divorce.[121]

Retirement pension entitlement could be divided by periodical payments as well as lump-sum payments upon divorce. Retirement pension recipient spouse can pay to the other spouse a certain proportion of the monthly retirement pension payment at a regular interval. If retirement pension entitlement is divided by the annuity method, however, a special characteristic should be taken into account: its amount cannot be specified, unlike other general properties, since retirement pension recipient spouse's remaining life span cannot be ascertained. Such a special characteristic could raise a problem in that uniform division proportion may not be equitable allowing for contribution to retirement pension entitlement and other general properties as a whole in view of all circumstances considered in property division. Then, it is reasonable to ascertain division proportion individually by distinguishing RP entitlement from other general properties: retirement pension division proportion shall be decided by taking into account the degree of other spouse's actual cooperation and contribution and all other circumstances such as the proportion of practical length of marriage among the whole employment period, job duties, division of homemaking or child care burdens, etc.[122]

On recent legislative interventions after these en banc decisions, the divorced spouse's public official pension or private school teacher's pension accumulated during the period of marriage over five years shall be divided in half to a spouse over sixty years old, who claims division of pension within three years from the time when the former spouse becomes an old-age beneficiary from Jan. 1, 2016.[123] However, in the case of Military Retirement Pension Act which has no similar direct provisions, the court can order the retirement pension recipient spouse to make payment for the benefit of a pensioner's spouse as and when such payments fall due on retirement on the condition that a pensioner survives. A wise and cautious legislative solution is required in order to treat the pensions fairly.

---

121 Supreme Court en banc Decision [S. Ct.] 2013Meu2250, July 16, 2014 (S. Kor.).

122 Supreme Court en banc Decision [S. Ct.] 2012Meu2888, July 16, 2014 (S. Kor.).

123 See *Kongmuwŏnyŏn'gŭmbŏp* [Public Official Pension Act] Act No. 13387, 22. June, art. 46-3 (S. Kor.) and *Sahakyŏn'gŭmbŏp* [Pension for Private School Teacher's and Staff Act] Act No. 13561, 15. Dec, 2015, art. 42 (S. Kor.). The two amended provisions took effect on Jan. 1, 2016.

New Property: Income Enhancing Licenses and Degrees

The issue of new property is whether a degree or license, such as medical doctor or advocate that will enhance the earning capacity of a spouse should be considered as marital property. The majority of the courts hold that income-enhancing license is not marital property, but they do not deny the right of the non-license spouse from being reimbursed for all reasonable expenses contributed towards obtaining the license. They take such factors into account in deciding division ratio as a whole in view of all circumstances considered in property division, relying on fairness.[124] In a case where a wife contributed to her husband becoming a university professor of economics in the hope that future benefits would accrue for her, and where the marriage ended before she got such benefits, the Court concluded that she deserved to be reimbursed for her sacrifice and effort according to a designated division ratio.

D Division Ratio

Proportion as to the Whole Accumulated Property

The determination of a division ratio is left to the judge's discretion, while the existence and value of property as object of division requires strict proof. Under 839-2(2) of KCC, property division ratio refers not to the degree of contribution to individual property, but proportion as to the whole accumulated property in view of the degree of contribution and all other circumstances. Thus the court is not allowed to attribute a different division proportion to individual divisible property without a reasonable basis. There are two exceptions for reasonable basis.

Different Proportion to Retirement Pension Entitlement

As discussed above, retirement pension entitlement's amount cannot be specified upon divorce, unlike other general properties, since retirement pension recipient spouse's remaining life span cannot be ascertained. Thus, applying one uniform division proportion through considering contribution to retirement pension entitlement and other general properties as a whole may not be equitable. Then, it may be reasonable to ascertain division proportion individually by distinguishing entitlement from other general properties: retirement pension division proportion shall be decided by taking into account the other spouse's actual cooperation, contribution degree and all other circumstances such as the proportion of practical length of marriage given the

124 Supreme Court Decision [S. Ct.] 98Meu 213, June 12, 1998 (S. Kor.).

whole employment period, job duties, division of homemaking or child care burdens, etc.[125]

As noted earlier, in case of debt exceeding property or the decrease of property by debt division, support after divorce as well as liquidation of property acquired in marriage shall be considered. In other words, a ratio of negative property division is unlike a ratio of positive property division where a uniform rate is applied depending on contribution to property. Therefore, total circumstances shall be considered like debt incurrence, use, contents, amount, marital life, economic activity ability, future prospect, and its division method.[126]

Equitable Factors

The courts allow for equitable factors in deciding the division ratio for the distribution of property. Factors include: (1) the duration of the marriage, (2) the age and health of both parties, (3) domestic sacrifices of the party seeking division, (4) contributions of one spouse made to the career or career potential of the other spouse, (5) Any direct or indirect contribution made to the acquisition of such marital property by the party not having title, including joint efforts or expenditures and contributions and services as a spouse, parent, wage earner and homemaker, and (6) the impossibility or difficulty of evaluating any component asset or any interest in a business, corporation or profession, and the economic desirability of retaining such asset or interest. According to a recent regression analyses, the duration of the marriage, the age of husband and wife, a working status of husband and wife, and the scale of net property turned out to be decisive factors for property division.[127] The marital period is one of the important factors considered by the court: the longer the duration of marriage is, the more the ratio of property division. For long term marriages over thirty years, a fifty-fifty division of marital assets is the norm. The division percentage of property for a working wife is higher than that of a full-time housewife. The scale of property makes an impact in the opposite direction: for small wealth, the formation of marital property was appraised by joint efforts and the marital property is distributed equally for the support after divorce; while for large wealth the ratio is low. This data shows that the average ratio of property division for the plaintiff is 46%. The number of cases

125 Supreme Court en banc Decision [S. Ct.] 2012Meu2888, July 16, 2014 (S. Kor.).

126 Supreme Court en banc Decision [S. Ct.] 2010Meu4071, 4088, June 20, 2013 (S. Kor.).

127 Park Min-Soo, Lee Dong-Jin, Oh Joung-Il, *Ihon Hu Chaesanbunharŭi Piyul Mit Ihon Wijaryoŭi Kyŏlchŏng [The Ration of Marital Division and the Amount of Divorce Pain and Suffering Damages: A Statement Analysis of Korean Courts' Decision from 2009 to 2011]*, *in* Kajokpŏbyŏn'gu [Korean Journal of Family Law], Vol. 28-1, 124 (2014).

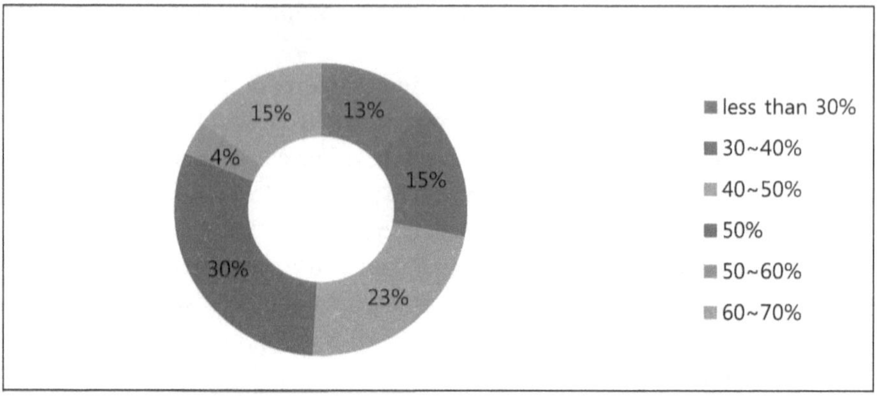

FIGURE 3 *Portion of property division 2009–2011.*
SOURCE: PARK MIN-SOO ET AL., *IHON HU CHAESANBUNHARŬI PIYUL MIT IHON WIJARYOŬI KYŎLCHŎNG [THE RATION OF MARITAL DIVISION AND THE AMOUNT OF DIVORCE PAIN AND SUFFERING DAMAGES: A STATEMENT ANALYSIS OF KOREAN COURTS' DECISION FROM 2009 TO 2011], IN* KAJOKPŎBYŎN'GU [KOREAN JOURNAL OF FAMILY LAW], VOL. 28-1, 120 (2014).

TABLE 2 *Portion of property division by period, 1998, 2005 and 2013*

<table>
<tr><th></th><th>0~30%</th><th>31~40%</th><th>41~49%</th><th>50%</th><th>51~60%</th><th>61~80%</th><th>81~100%</th></tr>
<tr><td>1998</td><td>35</td><td>35.1</td><td colspan="2">24.5</td><td>0</td><td>2.2</td><td>3.2</td></tr>
<tr><td>2005</td><td>16.8</td><td>28.0</td><td>5.9</td><td>29.9</td><td>2.8</td><td>1.9</td><td>4.7</td></tr>
<tr><td>2013</td><td>12.1</td><td>14.3%</td><td>15.9</td><td>33.7</td><td>9.5</td><td>10.5</td><td>3.8</td></tr>
</table>

SOURCE: SONG HYO-JEAN, JUN GYUNG-GUN, *IHONSHI CHAESANBUNHARE KWANHAN CH'OEGŬN P'ALLYE PUNSŎK [RECENT KOREAN COURT DECISION ON MARITAL PROPERTY DIVISION ON DIVORCE], IN* KAJOKPŎBYŎN'GU [KOREAN JOURNAL OF FAMILY LAW], VOL. 28-1, 133–162 (2014).

in which equal distribution (50%:50%) between the couple reached as high as 30% around in 2009 to 2011 (Figure 3).[128]

Another empirical research of 2013 proves that the ratio of property distribution for women has increased since 1998 (Table 2)[129] shows that the number

128 *Id.*

129 Song Hyo-Jean, Jun Gyung-Gun, *Ihonshi Chaesanbunhare Kwanhan Ch'oegŭn P'allye Punsŏk [Recent Korean Court Decision on Marital Property Division on Divorce], in* Kajokpŏbyŏn'gu [Korean Journal of Family Law], Vol. 28-1, 133–162 (2014).

of cases in which equitable distribution (40~50%) between the couple rise from 24.5% in 1998, through 35.8% in 2005, to 49.6% in 2013. It could be interpreted that women's right in divorce has been improved.

On the other side, the Korean courts do not seem to consider awarding the marital home to the custodial parent as in other countries. However, if there are sufficient assets to offset the home, the court should award ownership of the marital home to the custodial parent. Even if not, the court should award the custodial parent the exclusive right to occupy and use the marital home for a specific period of time, at least until the youngest child reaches eighteen years old.

Right to Revoke Fraudulent Act for Preserving Claim for Property Division

Transferring assets to a third party for less than what they are worth will result in severe sanctions against the offending party. The court could award a higher percentage of the remaining assets to the other spouse. In addition, a separate action to revoke a fraudulent act may be filed against the other party to undo the transfer. When a party has performed any juristic act which has a property right for its subject, with the knowledge that it would prejudice the other party's exercise of a claim for property division, the other party may file a lawsuit demanding a revocation of such act and a recovery of damages.[130]

IV *Pain and Suffering Damages*

Pain and suffering damages upon divorce played a larger role before a property division system was established in 1990. An innocent spouse can file a damages against a liable spouse for economic damage as well as non-economic damage (articles 843 and 806 of KCC). In deciding amount of pain and suffering damages, the court considers factors as follows: (1) details and degree of fault, (2) the ground and liability of dissolution of marriage, (3) the age of innocent spouse, (4) financial status and standard of living (5) the duration of the marriage, (6) identity status of academic career and job, (7) number of children and support relation, (8) the possibility of remarriage.[131] Duration of marriage, gender of innocent spouse and infidelity as a reason of divorce

130 Art. 839-3 of KCC.

131 See Supreme Court Decision [S. Ct.] 68Meu5, March 5, 1968 (S. Kor.); Supreme Court Decision [S. Ct.] 75Meu 33, Feb. 10, 1976 (S. Kor.); Supreme Court Decision [S. Ct.] 87Meu100, Oct. 13, 1981 (S. Kor.); Supreme Court Decision [S. Ct.] 87Meu55, 56, Oct. 28, 1987 (S. Kor.); Supreme Court Decision [S. Ct.] 92Meu 143, Mai 27, 1993 (S. Kor.).

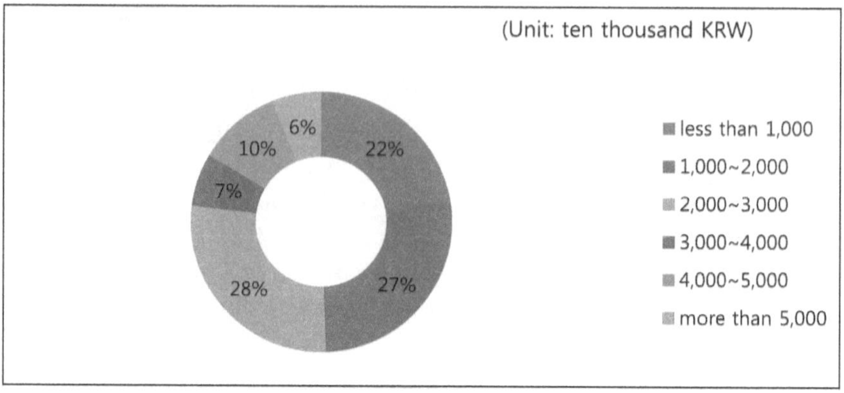

FIGURE 4 *Amount of pain and suffering damages 2009–2011.*
SOURCE: PARK MIN-SOO ET AL., *IHON HU CHAESANBUNHARŬI PIYUL MIT IHON WIJARYOŬI KYŎLCHŎNG* [*THE RATION OF MARITAL DIVISION AND THE AMOUNT OF DIVORCE PAIN AND SUFFERING DAMAGES: A STATEMENT ANALYSIS OF KOREAN COURTS' DECISION FROM 2009 TO 2011*], *IN* KAJOKPŎBYŎN'GU [KOREAN JOURNAL OF FAMILY LAW], VOL. 28-1, 121 (2014).

are important determinants for the amount of compensation for pain and suffering.[132] The average pain and suffering is 26.8 million won (Figure 4).[133]

In a recent en banc decision, however, the Korean Supreme Court denied the betrayed spouse's pain and suffering damages against the betraying spouse on the basis that the act of infidelity was committed after their spousal relationship had already been irretrievably dissolved.[134] It means that the act of unchastity during the irremediable breakdown of a marriage is not a matter of tort. In principle, the ruling confirmed that whether the couple's divorce is being processed does not have an impact to this conclusion, as long as there are irreconcilable differences between them. This decision was released before en banc decision concerning fundamental issue of fault-based divorce or no-fault divorce was passed, and right after this decision, the Constitutional Court repealed the punishment of adultery. So numerous Korean commentators thought the Supreme Court foreshadowed a change to no-fault divorce law through this decision. They were not correct in their guess as the Supreme Court affirmed the preexisting case law that does not allow a family court

132 Park Min-Soo, Lee Dong-Jin, Oh Joung-Il, *supra* note 127, at 126.
133 *Op.cit.*, at 127.
134 Supreme Court en banc Decision [S. Ct.] 2011Meu2997, Nov. 20, 2014 (S. Kor.).

to grant a judicial divorce in response to a petition by an at-fault spouse on September 15, 2015.[135]

V *Conclusion*

How to settle the marital property equally or equitably between the spouses upon divorce is one of the key issues in divorce from an economic point of view. In this chapter, we have reviewed the major legal developments in property division through enlarging or reconceptualizing the nature of marital property. As to the threshold question of whether or not pension entitlement constitute marital assets, the Korean Supreme Court determined that a public official's retirement and pension entitlement should be an object of property division, by overruling the precedent case law taking it into account as mere "other circumstance" for evaluating contents and method of property division. It was a huge breakthrough for further development of Korean divorce laws. This decision served as a momentum that triggered a legislative intervention to resolve this controversial issue. The case that held that a spouse of a national pension recipient gets half of the amount accumulated during the marriage period caused the reform of two other laws concerning pension in the same way last year as mentioned above. Now we will turn another axis of the two economic consequences of divorce, the financial effect on child upon divorce.

Part V Effect of Divorce on Child

I *Overview*

Roughly ninety thousand children were impacted by divorce in 2014 in Korea: the number of couples who have minor child have declined every year since 2004. (Table 3). The ratio of divorce with minor child reached 68.5% in 2004; but it decreased to 49.5% in 2014 (Figure 5). Legal decisions on custody, visitation, and child support of these children have enormous and far-ranging effects: these decisions as well as their enforcement shall influence social chances, emotional experiences and economic status of children after divorce. Parents' divorce shall mold and color their children's entire lives, especially if they are confronted with of the divorce of their parents when they are minors. Thus, divorce laws should take such effect into account and focus on securing child support after divorce.

First step is to decide who will be the custodian. This question is complicated in that custody and parental authority are different in Korean law. Second

135 Supreme Court [S. Ct.], 2013Meu568, Sept. 15, 2015 (S. Kor.).

TABLE 3 *Number of divorces by minor child 2004–2014* (Unit: 1,000)

	2004	Percent	2005	2006	2007	2008	2009	2010	2011	2012	2013	2014	Percent	Year-on-year percent change
Total*	138.9	(100.0)	128.0	124.5	124.1	116.5	124.0	116.9	114.3	114.3	115.3	115.5	100.0	0.2
Have minor child	91.1	(68.5)	81.2	75.7	72.8	63.0	68.5	62.9	60.1	60.3	59.0	57.2	49.5	−3.1
One	39.1	(28.7)	35.0	33.4	32.2	28.5	31.5	30.0	29.0	29.9	30.1	30.0	25.9	−0.5
Two	45.5	(35.0)	40.2	36.9	35.2	29.8	31.9	28.3	26.7	26.2	24.7	23.3	20.2	−5.4
More than three	6.5	(4.8)	6.0	5.5	5.4	4.7	5.1	4.6	4.4	4.1	4.2	3.9	3.3	−8.4
Have no minor child	46.4	(29.5)	45.4	48.2	50.9	52.9	55.1	53.7	53.9	53.7	56.1	58.1	50.3	3.5

* Including 'Unidentified'
SOURCE: STATISTICS KOREA, MARRIAGE AND DIVORCE STATISTICS IN 2014, 20 (2015).

one is how to maintain the relation with the children and non-rearing parent. This is closely connected to the visitation right. Third decision would be about how the responsibility should be shared between rearing parent and non-rearing parent. Last but not least, the enforcement of these court decisions, especially how to let the non-rearing parents pay periodically or how to collect over-due support effectively.

There have been remarkable developments concerning child support after divorce in Korean divorce law recently. As discussed above, pre-reform law for consensual divorce had not require any decision on child fostering matters, and as a result, the most important issues like custody, visitation and child support

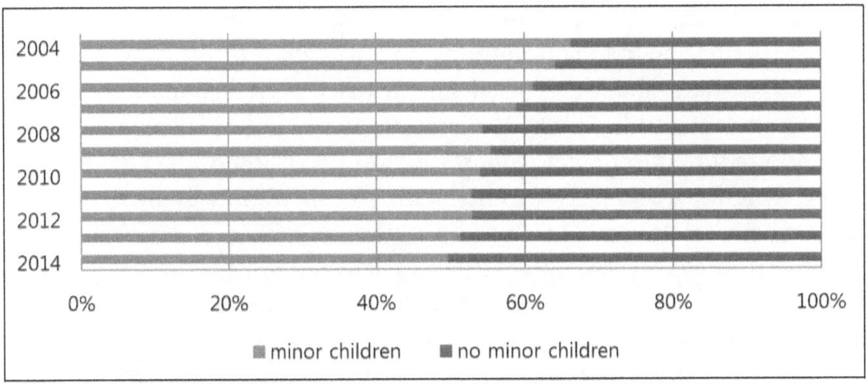

FIGURE 5 *Ratio of divorce by minor child 2004–2014.*
SOURCE: STATISTICS KOREA, MARRIAGE AND DIVORCE STATISTICS IN 2014, 20 (2015)

expenses were debated in a flurry as a post-divorce problem. Due to reform, the decision between the husband and wife including the three issues above became an essential prerequisite for the court's confirming couple's divorce intention, and the protocol of child support agreement made upon consensual divorce has the same legal force as the court's decision upon judicial divorce.

However, the so-called 'deadbeat dad,' who would not pay the child support expenses notwithstanding the courts' decision, became social problem. The children have been "the tragic victims of the present system of inadequate and unpaid child support."[136] To solve this problem, various measures to strengthen a collection of the support were introduced through a reform of the Korean Civil Code in 2012, a revision of the Family Procedure in 2013, and an establishment of Act on Securing Execution of Support Fee and Support in 2015. We will review as follows.

II *Custodian and Visitation Rights*

One of the most important issues for the children upon divorce is a custody-decision. The legal framework of child custody in Korea needs supplementary explanation. Historically, only the father could have a parental authority, which means a right to represent his minor child legally as well as a fundamental obligation to protect and foster the child. In reality where the mother raised the child after divorce, however, there was a need to grant a legal status to the

136 Lenore J. Weitzman, *supra* note 14, 323 ff.

mother fostering the child. Thus, the concept of "custody" appeared in the KCC. "Custody" and "parental authority" in Korea could be the counterparts to "physical custody" and "legal custody" in the U.S. During their marriage, principally the parental authority shall be jointly exercised by both parents, since the 1977 reform introduced joint parental authority.[137] If the parents fail to reach an agreement on who has a parental authority, the Family Court shall determine it upon the request of the parties. In cases of judicial divorce, the Family Court shall *ex officio* determine the person with authority.

Generally a custodian is a person with parental authority, but the former and the latter need not necessarily be the same:[138] there could be a custodian without parental authority and a non-custodian with parental authority; sole custody and joint authority; or joint custody; or split custody. Then who determines? In consensual divorce, the parties shall determine by agreement, and if the agreement cannot be made, then the family court shall decide upon the request of the party or *ex officio*. Whereas in judicial divorce, the court shall designate the custodian and person with parental authority at its discretion.

What are the criteria in deciding custody and parental authority? The KCC provides that "When the Family Court determines custodian, priority shall be given to the welfare of a child." There are several doctrines: maternal preference called the "tender year presumptions," the "primary caretaker presumptions" for continuity of fostering,[139] and the "best interest of the child." The Korean Family Court shall consider all relevant factors including: the sex and age of the minor child, the wishes of the parents; the wishes of the child; the interaction and interrelationship of the child with his/her parents, and the presence of financial power of parents.[140] Once custody is validly established, it needs justifiable reasons to modify the current custody status.[141]

A parent not granted custody of a child is entitled to visitation rights, unless the court finds that the visitation would harm the child's emotional or mental health. Visitation rights have been recognized to the parent who does not

137 See art. 909 of KCC. The problem of gender inequality still remained, however, in that when the parents failed to reach an agreement, the father would exercise paternal authority under the KCC of 1977. Thus, it was revised that when the parents failed to reach an agreement, the Family Court shall determine paternal authority upon the request of the parties under the 1990 reform.

138 See Supreme Court [S. Ct.] 2011Meu4719, April 13, 2012 (S. Kor.).

139 See generally, Sanford. N. Katz, Family Law in America 104–106 (2003).

140 See Supreme Court [S. Ct.] 2009Meu1458, 1465, May 13, 2010 (S. Kor.).

141 See Supreme Court [S. Ct.] 2008Meu380, May 8, 2008 (S. Kor.); Supreme Court [S. Ct.] 2008Meu3105, April 9, 2009 (S. Kor.); Supreme Court [S. Ct.] 2009Meu1458, 1465, May 13, 2010 (S. Kor.).

have custody of a minor child after divorce since the 1990 reform, and to the child since 2007 reform in Korea.[142] Visitation rights may be determined by the agreement of the parties or by a court order. Visitation usually means regular meetings, alternate weekends, one overnight mid-week, alternating holidays, or correspondence. The family court, however, may restrict or exclude such visitation rights upon the request of the party or ex officio, if it is required for the welfare of children.[143] Visitation is very important in that it is closely related to voluntary performance of child support of a non-custodial parent. When a noncustodial parent encounters problems in exercising visitation rights, the parent may stop paying child support to change the custodial parent's behavior. However, the courts do not recognize this as a valid reason for withholding support, as visitation and support are separate and discrete issues.

III *Child Support Calculation Guidelines*

It is not easy to evaluate the adequacy of child support awards, in the sense that child support expenses vary according to the family's living standards, the parents' salary, or region. Inflation and increase of education fees as children grow up should be considered. There could be three standards: the first one is the actual costs of raising children, and this is called as "cost approach"; second one is to decide the reasonableness to the payer's financial resources, and this is called as "income sharing approach"; third one involves fairly apportioning the responsibility between father and mother.[144] However, the method of determining the child support is not expressly stated in Korean law.

In practice, the guidelines of child-rearing expenses issued by the Seoul Family Court are referred when the Korean courts order the amount of child support payment.[145] The Seoul Family Court set forth uniform guidelines in the form of a calculation table for determining the amount of child support payment in March 2012 for the first time and it modified the guidelines in

142 Art. 837-2 (1) of KCC. Unlike many countries where the grandparents or other relatives have extensive visitation rights, only the non-custodian parent and the child have such rights in Korea. Legislative intervention is needed to enlarge the scope of visitation right to the grand parents or siblings for the best interest of the child.

143 Art. 837-2 (2) of KCC.

144 See generally, Katz, *supra* note 139, at 106–108.

145 The Seoul Family Court has unique and leading-edge standing in system of organizing courts, in the sense that it had been the only family court since 1963 for more than forty years in Korea: Four additional family courts were set up in *Busan* (2011), in *Daegu, Gwangju* and *Daejeon* (2012).

TABLE 4 *Basis to child-rearing expenses 2014 (Unit: 1000 KRW)*

Age of Child \ Net Family Income	0–199	200–299	300–399	400–499	500–599	600–699	700–799
0~2	526	653	761	906	1,012	1,106	1,526
3~5	490	705	878	1,008	1,238	1,334	1,759
6~11	533	708	902	1,059	1,202	1,371	1,906
12~14	604	755	947	1,095	1,305	1,520	2,046
15~17	608	844	1,115	1,204	1,424	1,668	2,227
18~20	959	1,185	1,303	1,361	1,728	1,974	2,221
21~22	975	1,132	1,308	1,636	1,815	2,046	2,339

SOURCE: THE SEOUL FAMILY COURT ANNOUNCED IN 2014. 5. 30.

June 2014.[146] These guidelines are not legally binding, but they serve as a key reference for determination of support payment by the Korean courts, and as a counterpart of the so-called *Dusseldorfer* Table used by German courts. Before these guidelines were issued, there were critics pointing out the discrepancies among the courts, since each court individually evaluated the support amount at its own discretion and this made it hard for the parties to predict with any measure of certainty the child support amounts.

Table 4 reveals that the children's age and the net family income are two key criteria in deciding the amount of child rearing expenses. First, it divides seven groups according to the amount of net family income. The income here is the sum total of salary, operating income, rent income, interest income, and pension. The first group earns income less than 1,990,000KRW (approximately 1,650USD), while the seventh group earns income more than 8,000,000KRW (6,600USD) per month. Second, the age of children to be supported are divided into seven groups from zero-to-two year of age to twenty-one-to-twenty-two year of age. The Table shows that the older the children get the more support is needed. It is noteworthy that this Table provides the information of expenses even after the children reach eighteen year of age, the age of major; in general, the time of economic independence from parents are getting late, for example, almost college students depend on their parents in tuition fees as well as living

146 This Table is roughly estimated to reflect a reality compared to the previous table; the average amount increased and the distinction of city and country became one of the factors to decide the amount, not criteria of distinction.

expenses in Korea; and the support expenses between twenty-one-to-twenty-two year of age, the last interval in the Table is the highest. This standard of average amount of child support expenses is based on four people family, and it does not correspond to real child support payment imposed to non-rearing parent. Other factors such as the number of children to be supported, whether the children reside in city or in country, or whether they need high-priced treatments are taken into account.

IV *Enforcement of Child Support Obligations*

The enforcement of child support obligations have developed from private to national remedies. To enhance collection of child support, various measures to strengthen a collection of the support were introduced through a reform of the Korean Civil Code in 2012, a revision of the Family Procedure in 2013, and an establishment of Act on Securing Execution of Support Fee and Support in 2015.[147]

The Protocol of the Child Support as a Title of Execution

The Protocol of Child Support made during the process of certifying the consensual divorce is recognized as a title of execution.[148] With Protocol, the rearing parent can execute on the property of the non-rearing parent in default. Thus, the rearing parent does not need to bring a lawsuit against the former spouse in order to obtain a title of execution such as a judgment of the court.

Order to Submit a Property List and Property Inquiry

Another special measure made it easier for a creditor of a child support to look for the non-rearing parent's property. Unlike in general civil cases in which orders to submit a property list are granted only after a creditor already got the title of execution, the order to submit a property list for child support enforcement can be granted as long as a child support suit is pending. The family court may order the defendant to submit a catalogued list stating all his or her property status either ex officio or upon request by the relevant party.[149] If the defendant who received this order rejects to submit a property list or submits a false property list without any justifiable reason, the court can impose a fine for negligence.[150]

147 See Jinsu Yune, *supra* note 49, at 247–261.

148 Art. 836-2 (5) of KCC & *Gasasosongbeob* [Family Procedure Act], Act. No. 4300, Dec. 31, 1990, art. 41 (S. Kor.).

149 *Gasasosongbeob* [Family Procedure Act], Act. No. 4300, Dec. 31, 1990, art. 48-2 (S. Kor.).

150 *Id.*, art. 67-2.

If the court finds the property list submitted as insufficient, the court may inquire about the property under the title of the defendant to public agencies, financial institutions, or other organizations that have computer network access to the credit information.[151] If the head of an agency or organization who received this inquiry submits false materials or rejects to submit material without any justifiable reason, the court can impose a fine.[152]

Order for Direct Payment of Child Support

An epoch-making system is the courts' issuing a direct payment order to the employer of the non-rearing parent in default.[153] Two conditions are required to apply this order for direct payment: the applicant should have a title of execution; also, the debtor obliged to pay the child support periodically had to fail to pay in more than two occasions without just grounds. If these conditions are met, the court shall order the debtor's employer that regularly pays wages to the debtor and pays withholding income tax. Then the recipient employer should deduct the amount of child support from the debtor's wages and pay the deducted amount directly to the creditor. If the employer disobeys this order without any justifiable reason, a fine shall be imposed against the employer.[154]

By this order, the right of the debtor against the employer is transferred to the creditor, and the right of the creditor against the debtor is extinguished simultaneously: as a result, the creditor has a risk of losing his or her right when the employer becomes insolvent.[155] Nonetheless, this measure has considerably alleviated the burden of the creditor regarding the execution of child support when the child support debtor is an employee.

Order to Offer Security and Lump Sum Payment Order

However, a direct payment order above mentioned will be useless when the child support debtor is not an employee; in such a case, the court may order the debtor to offer security to guarantee its implementation.

The orders to provide a considerable security shall be issued in two levels. The first one is the order the court issues when it sentenced the periodical payment of a child support.[156] This order shall be issued ex officio, if the court considers it is necessary. The second one can be issued when the debtor

151 *Id.*, art. 48–3.
152 *Id.*, art. 67-3.
153 *Id.*, art. 63-2.
154 *Id.*, art. 67.
155 Yune commented on this risk (Jinsu Yune, *supra* note 49, at 255).
156 *Gasasosongbeob* [Family Procedure Act], Act. No. 4300, Dec. 31, 1990, art. 63-3 (1) (S. Kor.).

fails to perform its liability without any justifiable grounds.[157] In this case, the application of the credit with a title of execution is required. The creditor has a pledge right upon the provided security. The object of security can be cash, negotiable instrument, or bank bond or insurance company bond. If the debtor does not obey this order without any justifiable reason, the court may impose a fine.[158]

If the child support obligor subject to this order fails to provide security, the court may order the obligor to make a lump sum payment upon the request of the creditor.[159] This lump sum payment order itself is not a title of execution. Therefore, the efficiency of lump sum payment is questionable.

Detention Order

If the obligor required to make a lump sum payment does not perform its liability within 30 days, the court shall punish the obligor by detention until its payment is made within the limit of 30 days, upon the request of the creditor.[160] The effect of detention order appears powerful and prompt. There are several reported cases where non-custodial fathers were delinquent on their child support payments for years, and it was not until they were detained pursuant to a court order that they paid the arrears in full. Figure 6 shows that the dramatic

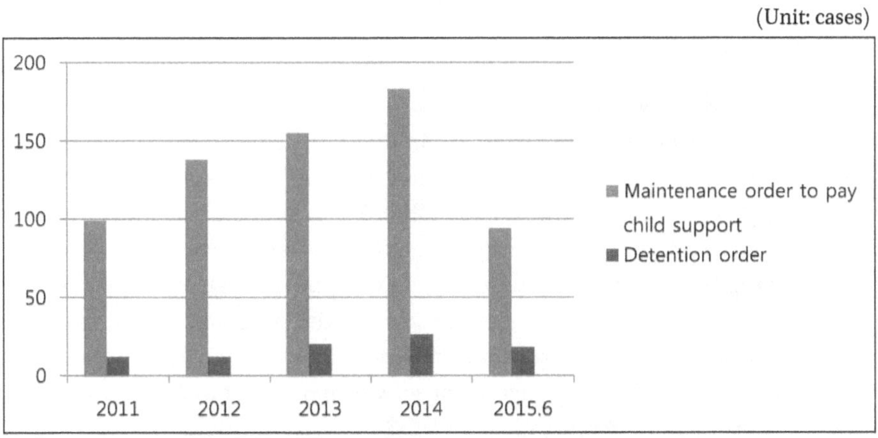

FIGURE 6 *Maintenance order to pay child support and detention order 2011–2015.6.* SOURCE: THE SEOUL FAMILY COURT (2015. 8. 19.).

157 *Id.*, art. 63-3 (2).
158 *Id.*, art. 67.
159 *Id.*, art. 63-3 (4).
160 *Id.*, art. 68 (1), item 3.

rise of the Seoul Family Court's maintenance order to pay child support and detention order. in last four and half years.

Assessment

All parents living apart from their children are obligated to share their income with their children. Besides the measures to strengthen collection of the support mentioned above, other enforcement techniques to enhance collection of past-due child support payments should be introduced: such as withholding wages, intercepting tax refunds, rejecting issuance of a passport, suspending driving license, freezing financial accounts and registering defaulting parent as credit defaulter. These measures are already taken in some states in U.S.: for example, every order of court shall contain an immediate order for the withholding of income, and the court shall, upon certification of the overdue support owed by the obligor, enter an immediate order prohibiting the release of those assets until further order of court, and where the obligor owes support in an amount equal to or greater than three months of the monthly support obligation, the court shall prohibit the issuance or renewal of a license or require the suspension of the license of the obligor by issuing an order directing any licensing authority in Pennsylvania (231 Pa. R.C.P. §1910, 23 Pa. C.S. §4355). Several bills for improving the existing mechanics of past-due child support, imposes an oversea travel ban to "the deadbeat dad" are pending in the National Assembly.[161]

V *Child Support Agency*

Belatedly, but wisely, state involvement in enforcing child support obligations started recently in Korea. On March 25, 2015, *Yangyukbi ihangkwalliwon* "Child Support Agency" was launched under the Ministry of Gender and Family (MOGEF), based on "Act on Securing Execution of Support Fee and Support," in order to support the implementation of child support expenses under a single parent.[162] As the minister of MOGEF expressed, the purpose of establishing it is to make the children-raising or non-raising parents have responsibility over the children through the support of the government, so that the children can grow in safety at any circumstance.

161 There are three different bills: bill proposed by a member of the National Assembly Seung-min Yu and others in 2015; bill proposed by a member of the National Assembly Cha-ik Lee and others in 2015; bill proposed by a member of the National Assembly Hyun-joo Min and others in 2015. Bill Information System of Republic of Korea, *available at* http://likms.assembly.go.kr/bill/jsp/BillSearchResult.jsp (last visited Jan. 10, 2016).

162 http://www.childsupport.or.kr/jsp/service_01.jsp.

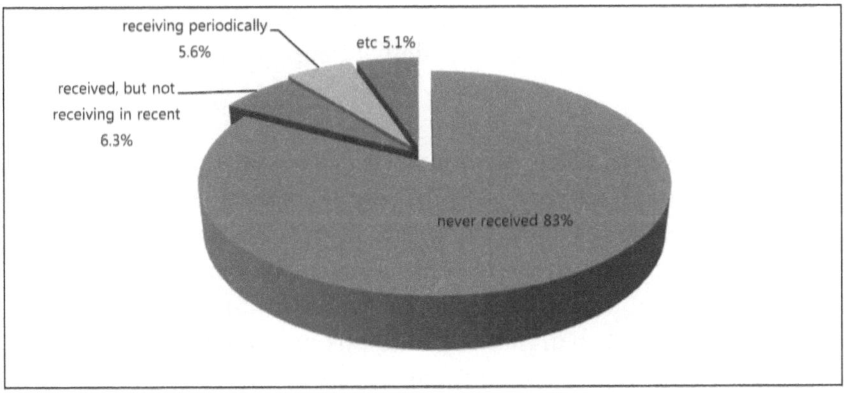

FIGURE 7 *Status of child support payment.*
SOURCE: THE MINISTRY OF GENDER AND FAMILY, REPORT OF SURVEY STUDY ON SINGLE (2013).

Despite court orders, non-rearing parents fail to pay in child support: more than three quarters of the rearing parents have not received the court-ordered support stably: only 24.3% of non-rearing parent pay periodically. What was worse, 83% of thirty nine millions of single-parent families had not been paid at all and 4.6% of them had never attempted to file a suit for executing child support (Figure 7).[163]

This high rate of unpaid and unenforced child support provided in the Table, shows the widespread wrong belief of the non-rearing parents that they cannot afford to pay the support and being a deadbeat parent is not a disgrace. The grounds of this intentional non-compliance could be explained in that there is an absence of social awareness, obligors would conceal their property, or procedures for filing a suit are burdensome.

One Stop Service

Child Support Agency provides customized and comprehensive support necessary for securing child support expenses: it includes counseling, agreement on child support arrangement, investigation on the address, work place, income and asset of debtor (non-rearing parent), demand for child support expenses and suit to secure implementation, credit collection, and monitoring on the payment of child support expenses. Any single parent, regardless of being divorced or unmarried, can apply for this service, and once an application is applied, the service continues until the child becomes an adult. This one-stop

163 The Ministry of Gender and Family, Report of Survey Study on single (2013).

service by the government will be a ladder of hope for the divorced rearing parent and his/her children who are suffering from economic deficiency, if it functions well.

Temporary and Limited Advance Child Support Payment

One of the important services of Child Support Agency is Advance Child Support Payment of State, though the providing period is temporary up to six months and the amount is limited to only 20,0000 KRW per month. Its beginning is humble, but it is noteworthy in the sense that it is a meaningful first step. The developed system in German, Belgium or some states in the U.S. will be a role model for Advance Child Support Payment.

Assessment

It is too early to evaluate the outcome of the Child Support Agency; however, its pioneering work on the collection of child support are nothing short of incredible, especially given the fact that it is only eight months old.[164] On the first day it opened, more than three thousands and four hundreds peoples called into its hotline. For eight months, 5,673 applications were received after 27,897 cases were consulted; a whopping about 20,0000,0000 KRW (approximately 1,650,000 USD) of child support were collected.

VI *Proposals for Reform*

There have been remarkable developments concerning child support after divorce in Korean divorce laws recently as we have reviewed in this chapter, but it is still inadequate and insufficient. The main debate here is how the responsibility should be shared between rearing parent, non-rearing parent and the society as a whole.[165] The legislative intervention is still required to secure the children after divorce.

There are several proposals for future reform to strengthen collection of support from a deadbeat parent. First, an exception to the rule of ban of attachment on salaries should be recognized for creditors of child support expenses. In principle, attaching the amount equivalent to the half of wages, pension, salary, bonus, and retirement pension is prohibited if they are less than the minimum living cost.[166] The National Basic Living Security Act set the

---

164 Statistics of the Child Support Agency (2015. 11. 30).

165 Lenore J. Weitzman & Mavis Maclean, Economic Consequences of Divorce: The International Perspective 187 (1992).

166 *Minsajipaengbeob* [Civil Execution Act], Act. No. 7358, Jan. 27, 2005, art. 246(1), item 4 (S. Kor.).

minimum living cost 1,500,000 KRW per month. However, treating the creditor of child support payments the same as a general third party creditor is contrary to justice; therefore an exception to this priciple should be granted, even though the half of wages is less than the minimum living cost. Second, the present law requiring the child support obligor's consent in order to investigate his or her location or the list of his or her property when there is not a title of execution should be modified. Third, for more effective enforcement of child support claims, an electronic filing system for child support payments should be introduced, and branch offices of the Child Support Agency should be expanded more extensively throughout the nation. Fourth, Advance Child Support Payment of State should be enlarged in terms of the amount and the period. Last but not least, the most urgent task is to increase public awareness of the disgrace of not paying child support.

Part VI Conclusion

If the essence of marriage is love, even after a marriage breaks down, the divorcing couple needs to own up to the responsibility as a consequence of love. The responsibility will result in a cash payment, because it is difficult to deny that "financial needs and means act as indicators for the underlying issues of independency and power, individualism, and collectivity in the family."[167] Upon divorce, marital property including marital home, marital debt and pension benefits shall be divided equitably between the spouses. Besides, if one spouse is responsible for the breakdown of conjugal relation, moral damages with monetary compensation should be granted to the innocent spouse. Moreover, when the children are born or adopted in their marital life, the non-custodian parent should pay child support periodically until they reach the adult age at least. In that sense, "Divorce is the one human tragedy that reduces everything to cash."[168] is an insightful definition that describes the economic nature of divorce concisely and precisely. This characteristic of being reduced to cash makes divorce a conundrum in economic sense.

Furthermore, in evaluating the amount of property division and the child support payment upon divorce, regular cash income become much more important, as Mary Ann Glendon pointed out earlier that "the emphasis has shifted from rights in traditional property to the issue of rights in a spouse's

---

167 Lenore J. Weitzman & Mavis Maclean, *supra* note 165, at 9.

168 Rita Mae Brown, Sudden Death, (1988).

earning power and benefit."[169] The recent en banc decision in which the pension is newly recognized as object of property division, and subsequent revision of relevant pension laws which grant the divorced spouse the equal pension entitlement that has been accumulated during marriage, deserve to be highly evaluated. It is also noteworthy to see a belated but wise establishment of the state agency to enforce child support obligations and its soft landing.

Given the globalization of Family Law, the dilemma facing the world is almost the same. How to protect or support the divorced parent and children who are in disadvantaged economic position after divorce, securing freedom to divorce under high divorce rate? This concern is deeply related not only to the result of divorce but also to the condition and procedures of divorce. Korea might be seen in a negative light of going counter to the current of globalization of family law, in the sense that Korea sticks to fault-based divorce. However, the main reason of not admitting no-fault policy is that preconditions of systems for financially protecting the spouse and children after divorce are not yet satisfied in Korea. Then, it is confirmed that the goal of Korean divorce laws is the same as that of other countries' laws. Moreover, more than three quarters of divorce cases are made through "consensual divorce" in Korea, which guarantees the freedom to divorce and furthermore, lowers the pressure for no-fault divorce.

Meanwhile, the public sentiments towards divorce as well as the influence of Korean customs and culture should be considered carefully in lawmaking. Still, the Confucian view of divorce is prevalent among Korean people, especially the elite and the elder people from the countryside. Paradoxically, the fact that the recent sharp increase of couples who divorce after more than thirty years of marriage reflect the following: elderly women have become freed from any concern over others' perception of them and from the sense of responsibility for their children who are fully grown and married.

The perception and practice of divorce, however, have been transformed by new social roles for men and women, by changing views of marriage and parenting, and by changes in intergenerational relations. Therefore, the trend toward no fault divorce regime will be inevitable in Korea. The recent seven-to-six en banc decision by the Supreme Court foreshadows there is not much time left to be faced with introducing no-fault divorce law in Korea.[170] We have

169 Mary Ann Glendon, The Transformation of Family Law 135 (1989).

170 See Park Bok-Soon, Lee Yeo-Bong, *supra* note 106, at 339. This empirical research shows public's sentiments as follows: 34% of Korean people think that the time is not yet ripe for introduction of no-fault divorce; 55% are willing to accept it limitedly provided that the other spouse is protected; only 10% agree an overall introduction of no-fault divorce.

to use this golden time for preparing protective measures for the divorced women and children, through legislative effort. First, based on the criteria used in discerning principle and exception by the Family Court when a responsible spouse files a divorce suit, a hardship clause should be enacted: the hardship clause would state that a divorce petition has to be rejected if the divorce would cause more hardship to the respondent than a dismissal of the divorce petition to the petitioner, if the marriage is exceptionally essential in the interest of minor children born to the marriage, or if the divorce would cause such significant stress on one spouse that the continuance of the marriage appears to be necessary despite the other spouse's will to dissolve the marriage.

Lastly, I can not avoid confessing we still have miles to go before the divorce laws secure true equality or fairness financially upon divorce.[171] Considering the reality that mother generally raises the children after the divorce, it is urgent to raise public recognition that becoming a deadbeat parent is disgraceful and paying child support after divorce is an inevitable duty. On the other hand, I think the time has come to discuss seriously the issues of how the responsibility should be shared between rearing parent, non-rearing parent and the society as a whole in our society. Advance Child Support Payment of State will be a meaningful starting point.

List of References

Western-language Sources

Agell, Anders, *Grounds and Procedures Reviewed, in* Economic Consequences of Divorce: The International Perspective (Weitzman & Maclean eds., 1992).

Basedow, Jurgen, Klaus. J. Hopt, & Reinhard Zimmermann (eds.), *The Max Planck Encyclopedia of European Private Law*, Vol. 1, Oxford (2012).

Brown, Rita Mae, *Sudden Death*, Bantan Book (1988).

Deuchler, Martina, *The Confucian Transformation of Korea, A Study of Society and Ideology*, Harvard (1992).

Fuess, Herald, *Divorce in Japan, Family, Gender, and the State, 1600–2000*, Stanford, CA: Stanford University Press (2004).

Glendon, Mary Ann, *The Transformation of Family Law*, Chicago and London: Chicago University Press (1989).

Glendon, Mary Ann, (ed.), *International Encyclopedia of Comparative Law*, Vol. IV: Persons and Family, Martinus Nijhoff Publishers (2007).

171 See Sanford N. Katz, *Individual Rights and Family Relationships, in* Cross Currents, 634 (Sanford N. Katz, John Eekelaar & Mavis Maclean ed., 2015).

González, Libertad & Tarja K. Viitanen, *The Effect of Divorce Laws on Divorce Rates in Europe, in* Sheffield Economic Research Paper Series (2006).

Hoffman, Saul D. & Greg J. Duncan, "What Are the Economic Consequences of Divorce?" in *Demography*, Vol. 25, No. 4, 641–645 (1988).

Holmes, Jr., Oliver Wendell, *The Common Law* (1881).

Katz, Sanford N., *Family Law in America* (2003).

Katz, Sanford N., *Individual Rights and Family Relationships, in* Cross Currents, (Sanford N. Katz, John Eekelaar & Mavis Maclean ed., 2015).

Krause, Harry D., "Comparative Family Law: Past Traditions Battle Future Trends—and Vice Versa," in *The Oxford Handbook of Comparative Law*, Oxford University Press (Reimann & Zimmermann eds., 2006).

Lowe, Nigel & Gillian Douglas, *Bromley's Family Law*, Oxford: Oxford University Press (2007).

Lee, Whasook, "Transformation of Korean Family Law," in *International Survey of Family Law 2008*, 239–254 (B. Atkin ed., Jordan Publishing Limited, 2008).

Malaurie, Philippe, et Hugues Fulchiron, *Droit Civil: La Famille,* Paris: Defrénois (2011).

Montesquieu, Charles Baron De, *The Spirit of the Laws* (Thomas Nugent trans., Cosimo Classics 2011) (1784).

Pahk, Induk, *September Monkey*, New York: Harper & Brothers (1954).

Pahk, Induk, *The Hour of the Tiger*, New York: Harper & Brothers (1954).

Pahk, Induk, *The Cock Still Crows*, Vantage Press, Incorporated (1977).

Park, Dong-Jin, "Korean Divorce Law: Can a Spouse Guilty of Marital Misconduct Get a Divorce without the Consent of the Other Spouse?" in *International Survey of Family Law 2012*, 313–335 (B. Atkin ed., Jordan Publishing Limited, 2012).

Peterson, Richard R., "A Re-Evaluation of the Economic Consequences of Divorce," in *American Sociological Review*, Vol. 61, No. 3, 528–536 (1996).

Voltaire, François-Marie, *Dictionnaire philosophique*, (Alain Pons ed., Gallimand 1994) (1764).

Wadlington & O'Brien, *Family Law in Perspective*, New York: Foundation Press (2012).

Weitzman, Lenore J., *The Divorce Revolution*, New York: Free press (1985).

Weitzman, Lenore J., & Mavis Maclean, *Economic Consequences of Divorce: The International Perspective*, New York: Clarendon Press·Oxford (1992).

Weitzman, Lenore J., "The Economic Consequences of Divorce Are Still Unequal: Comment on Peterson," in *American Sociological Review*, Vol. 61, No. 3, 537–538 (1996).

Yune, Jinsu, "Tradition and the Constitution in the Context of the Korean Family Law," in *Journal of Korean Law*, Vol. 5, No. 1, 194–212 (2005).

Yune, Jinsu, "The Reform of the Consensual Divorce Process and the Child Support Enforcement System in Korea," in *Journal of Korean Law*, Vol. 11, 247–261 (2012).

Korean-language Sources

Byun Hwha-soon et al., Ihon hu Yeoseongui Sahoegyeongjejeok Jiwibyeonhwa [Changing of Women's Socio-economic Status after Divorce], Hangukyeoseonggaebalyeonguwon (2006).

Chang Byung-In, *Chosŏnshidae Ihone Taehan Kyujewa Kŭ Shilsang [The Regulation and Real Facts of Divorce in Chosun Period]*, in Minsok'akyŏn'gu [Folklore Study] 37–72 (1999).

Cheong Ji-Won, *Chosŏnshidae Ihu Han'gugŭi Ihonjedoe Taehan Ilgoch'al [A Study on the Divorce System of Korea After Chosun Dynasty -Focusing Mainly on the Causes of the Divorce and Gender Equality-]*, in Kajokpŏbyŏn'gu [Korean Journal of Family Law], Vol. 27-2, 139–172 (2013).

Cho Jiman, *Chosŏnshidaeŭi Hyŏngsabŏp-Taemyŏngnyulgwa Kukchŏn*-[The Ming Code and the National Code as Criminanal Law in the Joseon Dynasty] (Kyounginmunhwasa 2007).

Chung Hae-eun, *Chosŏnhugi Ihonŭi Shilsanggwa Taemyŏngnyurŭi Chŏkyong [The Reality of Divorces in the latter half period of the Joseon dynasty, and the application of the Grand Ming Code]*, in Chosŏnhugi Ihonŭi Shilsanggwa Taemyŏngnyurŭi Chŏkyong [History and Reality], No. 75, 93–125 (2010).

Jung Kwanghyun, *Han'gukkajokpŏbyŏn'gu* [Korean Law of Family Relations and Successions] (Seoul University Press, INC. 1967).

Jin Kim & Yontaek Lee, *Geu Ttaen Geu Giri Wae I-ri Jobatdeongo* [Why the road was so narrow then] (Haenuri 2009).

Kim Joo-soo & Kim Sang-yong, *Ch'injoksangsokpŏp* [Family Law] (Beopmunsa, 11 ed., (2013).

Kim Hye-young et al., *Yeoseongui Ihongwa Bingon: Jikeobgwa Sodeukui Byeonhwareul Jungsimeuro [Women's Divorce and Poverty: Focusing on the changes in occupations and incomes], in* Gajokgwa Munhwa [Family and Culture], No. 20–2, 37–63 (2008).

Kukyŏk Kwansŭpchosabogosŏ [Survey Report on Customs] (Han'gukpŏpcheyŏn'guwŏn 1992).

Kwon Hee Jung, *Shikminji sidae hankook kagokeui byunhwa [The Change of Korean Family in the Colonial Period focusing on Divorce Case]*, in Bikyomunhwa younku, No. 11-2, 35–82 (2005).

Park Bok-Soon, *Hyŏbŭiihonjedoŭi Unyongshilt'ae Mit Kaesŏnbangan [The operation and improvement of the system for a divorce by agreement- Focused on the consideration period and counseling recommendation-]*, in Kajokpŏbyŏn'gu [Korean Journal of Family Law], Vol. 26-1, 1–24 (2012).

Park Bok-Soon, Lee Yeo-Bong, *Ŭishikchosarŭl T'onghan P'at'anjuŭi Toip Kanŭngsŏng Mosaek [Exploration of the Possibility of Acceptance Breakdown Divorce Principle through Surveys of Perceptions]*, in Kajokpŏbyŏn'gu [Korean Journal of Family Law], Vol. 27-1, 327–339 (2013).

Park Min-Soo, Lee Dong-Jin & Oh Jeung-Il, *Ihon Hu Chaesanbunharŭi Piyul Mit Ihon Wijaryoŭi Kyŏlchŏng [The Ration of Marital Division and the Amount of Divorce Pain and Suffering Damages: A Statement Analysis of Korean Courts' Decision from 2009 to 2011]*, in Kajokpŏbyŏn'gu [Korean Journal of Family Law], Vol. 28-1, 99–132 (2014).

Song Hyo-Jean, Jun Gyung-Gun, *Ihonshi Chaesanbunhare Kwanhan Ch'oegŭn P'allye Punsŏk [Recent Korean Court Decision on Marital Property Division on Divorce]*, in Kajokpŏbyŏn'gu [Korean Journal of Family Law], Vol. 28-1, 133–162 (2014).

Yune, Jinsu, *Honin'gwa Ihonŭi Pŏpkyŏngjehak* [Law and Economics of Marriage and Divorce], in Pŏpkyŏngjehak Yŏn'gu[Korean Journal of Law & Economics], Vol. 9-1, 35–69 (2012).

Yune, Jinsu, ed., Chuhaech'inchokpŏp, Vol. 1 (Pakyŏngsa 2015).

Yune, Jinsu, *Chŏnt'ongjŏk Kajokchedowa Hŏnbŏp [Traditional family system and the Constitution]*, in Minbŏpnon'go(IV), 89–126 (Pakyŏngsa 2009).

www.ingramcontent.com/pod-product-compliance
Lightning Source LLC
Chambersburg PA
CBHW031333230926
51848CB00001B/221
9789004323711